More TRUE STORIES

A HIGH-BEGINNING READER

THIRD EDITION

by Sandra Heyer

PEARSON
Longman

To legendary teacher Peggy Miles, in whose classroom thousands of learners have shared their true stories, and who changed the story of my professional life when I walked into her classroom in 1974.

More True Stories, Third Edition

Copyright © 2009 by Pearson Education, Inc.
All rights reserved.

Pearson Education, 10 Bank Street, White Plains, NY 10606

Staff credits: The people who made up the *More True Stories, Third Edition* team, representing editorial, production, design, and manufacturing, are Karen Davy, Nancy Flaggman, Dana Klinek, Michael Mone, Liza Pleva, Barbara Sabella, Loretta Steeves, Kim Teixeira, and Paula Van Ells.

Photo credits: Unit 1—Puppy Love (Hiroaki Yamashiro/courtesy of the *Ryukyu Shimpo*); **Unit 2**—Surprise! It's Your Wedding! (Courtesy of *the Bridlington Free Press*); **Unit 3**—Bad News, Good News (Apex Photo Agency); **Unit 4**—The Twins of Siam (Hulton-Deutsch Collection/Corbis); **Unit 5**—The Baby Exchange (*Folha de São Paulo*); **Unit 6**—The Ghost (Chris Collins/Corbis); **Unit 7**—Why Can't They Quit? (Sandra Heyer); **Unit 8**—Everybody's Baby (Scott Shaw/SIPA Press); **Unit 9**—Pay It Forward (Orlin Wagner/AP; M. Spencer Green/AP); **Unit 10**—Please Pass the Bird Brains (Brant Ward/*San Francisco Chronicle*); **Unit 11**—Margaret Patrick . . . Meet Ruth Eisenberg (Alan Zale/NYT Pictures); **Unit 12**—Finders Keepers? (Courtesy of Bruce Burns); **Unit 13**—The Husband (Steven Puetzer/Getty Image); **Unit 14**—The Auction (Lynn Ischay/*Columbus Dispatch*); **Unit 15**—Money to Burn (James Schnepf); **Unit 16**—The School and the Stamp (AP); **Unit 17**—A Long Fishing Trip (Peter Serling); **Unit 18**—The Surgeon (Eugene Louie/*San Jose Mercury News*); **Unit 19**—Customer Service? (Richard A. Lipski/*Washington Post*); **Unit 20**—The Mermaid Balloon (Gary Quiring); **Unit 21**—The Two Lives of Mary Sutton (Reprinted with the permission of Simon and Schuster from *Across Time and Death* by Jenny Cockell. Copyright 1993 by Jenny Cockell. Published in the UK and Commonwealth by Piatkus Books under the title *Yesterday's Children.* Map of Malahide reproduced with the permission of the Malahide Chamber of Commerce.); **Unit 22**—Two Strangers (Nick Brooks/AP. Train image from Clipart.com).

Text composition: Macmillan Publishing Solutions
Text font: 11.5/13 New Aster
Illustrations: Don Martinetti

Library of Congress Cataloging-in-Publication Data

Heyer, Sandra.
  More true stories : a high-beginning reader / by Sandra Heyer.—3rd ed.
    p. cm.
  ISBN 0-13-814342-0
  1. English language—Textbooks for foreign speakers. 2. Readers. I. Title.
  PE1128.H4358 2009
  428.6'4—dc22
                                                                    2009002080

Printed in the United States of America
3 4 5 6 7 8 9 10—VO39—13 12 11

Contents

Introduction

More True Stories is a high-beginning reader for students of English. It consists of 22 units based on human-interest stories adapted from newspapers and magazines. The vocabulary and structures used in the stories are carefully controlled to match those of a typical high-beginning class. At the same time, all attempts were made to keep the language natural.

In answer to those students who think some stories are too amazing to be true: Yes, the stories are true, to the best of our knowledge. A special "To the Teacher" section at the back of the book provides additional information about each story.

Following are some suggestions for using *More True Stories*. Teachers new to the field might find these suggestions especially helpful. Please remember that these are only suggestions. Teachers should, of course, feel free to adapt these strategies to best suit their teaching styles and their students' learning styles.

PRE-READING

Beneath the photo that introduces each unit are two sets of questions. The first set guides students as they describe the photo. The second set asks students to speculate on the content of the reading.

Each story in Levels 1 and 2 of the *True Stories* series—*Very Easy True Stories*, *All New Very Easy True Stories*, *Easy True Stories*, and *All New Easy True Stories*—is introduced with a sequence of drawings. Before students read, the teacher tells them the story while they look at the drawings. This Level 4 book has no pre-reading drawings. However, before students read, you can still tell them the gist of the story while drawing your own illustrations on the board. Only a few simple sketches can have a dramatic effect on subsequent reading comprehension, so this pre-reading activity is well worth the five or ten minutes you devote to it. If you're not skilled at drawing—and many of us are not—please see the drawing tips in the To the Teacher section at the back of the book. Also in the To the Teacher section are many suggestions for pre-, during-, and post-reading activities.

THE EXERCISES

Each unit has four types of exercises: vocabulary, comprehension, discussion, and writing. Students can complete the exercises individually, in pairs, in small groups, or with the whole class. The exercises can be completed in class or assigned as homework. At the back of the book, there is an answer key to the exercises.

VOCABULARY

The vocabulary exercises highlight words that ESL students identified as new and that could be clearly drawn, described, or defined. The exercises clarify meaning while giving students practice in establishing meaning through contextual clues. In the To the Teacher section at the back of the book, there are suggestions for supplemental vocabulary activities.

COMPREHENSION

The comprehension exercises test students' understanding of the story; more important, the exercises help students develop reading skills they will use throughout their reading careers—skills such as scanning, summarizing, identifying the main idea, and recognizing connectors and other rhetorical devices.

DISCUSSION

Most of the discussion exercises require students to complete a task—to fill in a chart, to interview a classmate, to draw a picture or a map—so that there is a concrete focus to the discussion. The task-centered exercises make it possible for students to talk without the direct supervision of the teacher, a necessity in large classes.

WRITING

Most of the writing exercises are structured: Students complete sentences, answer questions, and create lists. Students who are fairly accomplished writers may need more challenging assignments, such as writing short paragraphs or essays. Students who are less experienced writers may need to see some sample responses before they write.

The vocabulary, comprehension, discussion, and writing exercises are at approximately parallel levels; that is, they assume that students speak and write about as well as they read. Of course, that is not always the case. Please feel free to tamper with the exercises—to adjust them up or down to suit students' proficiency levels, to skip some, or to add some of your own.

Both the exercises and reading selections are intended to build students' confidence along with their reading skills. Above all, it is hoped that reading *More True Stories* will be a pleasure, for both you and your students.

UNIT 1

1. PRE-READING

Look at the picture.

▸ What is the dog doing?

Read the title of the story. Look at the picture again.

▸ Where do you think the dog is going?

▸ What do you think this story is about?

▸ Can you guess what happens?

Puppy Love

"Shiro! Shiro!"

Mr. and Mrs. Nakamura were worried. Their dog, Shiro, was missing. "Shiro!" they called again and again. Mr. and Mrs. Nakamura lived on a small island in Japan. They looked everywhere on the island, but they couldn't find Shiro.

The next day, Mr. Nakamura heard a noise at the front door. He opened the door, and there was Shiro. Shiro was very wet, and he was shivering.

A few days later, Shiro disappeared again. He disappeared in the morning, and he came back late at night. When he came back, he was wet and shivering.

Shiro began to disappear often. He always disappeared in the morning and came back late at night. He was always wet when he came back.

Mr. Nakamura was curious. "Where does Shiro go?" he wondered. "Why is he wet when he comes back?"

One morning Mr. Nakamura followed Shiro. Shiro walked to the beach, ran into the water, and began to swim. Mr. Nakamura jumped into his boat and followed his dog. Shiro swam for about two miles.[1] Then he was tired, so he climbed onto a rock and rested. A few minutes later, he jumped back into the water and continued swimming.

Shiro swam for three hours. Then he arrived at an island. He walked onto the beach, shook the water off, and walked toward town. Mr. Nakamura followed him. Shiro walked to a house. A dog was waiting in front of the house. Shiro ran to the dog, and the two dogs began to play. The dog's name was Marilyn. Marilyn was Shiro's girlfriend.

Marilyn lived on Zamami, another Japanese island. Shiro and the Nakamuras used to live on Zamami. Then the Nakamuras moved to Aka, a smaller island. They took Shiro with them. Shiro missed Marilyn very much and wanted to be with her. But he wanted to be with the Nakamuras, too. So, Shiro lived with the Nakamuras on the island of Aka and swam to Zamami to visit Marilyn.

People were amazed when they heard about Shiro. The distance from Aka to Zamami is two and a half miles,[2] and the ocean between the islands is very rough. "Nobody can swim from Aka to Zamami!" the people said.

Shiro became famous. Many people went to Zamami because they wanted to see Shiro. During one Japanese holiday, 3,000 people visited Zamami. They waited on the beach for Shiro. "Maybe Shiro will swim to Zamami today," they said. They all wanted to see Shiro, the dog who was in love.

[1] 3.2 kilometers
[2] 4 kilometers

2. VOCABULARY

Complete the sentences with the words below.

amazed	curious	~~missing~~	rough	shivering

1. Shiro disappeared. The Nakamuras looked everywhere for him, but they couldn't find him. Their dog was _____*missing*_____.

2. Shiro always came back at night. He was wet and cold, so he was _____.

3. "Where does Shiro go?" Mr. Nakamura wondered. He wanted to know. One day he followed his dog because he was _____.

4. Shiro's swimming surprised people. "Nobody can swim from Aka to Zamami!" they said. People were _____ when they heard about Shiro.

5. It was difficult for Shiro to swim because the ocean was _____.

3

3. COMPREHENSION

◆ **UNDERSTANDING THE MAIN IDEA**

Circle the letter of the best answer.

1. "Puppy Love" is about

   a. two islands in Japan.

   b. a Japanese holiday.

   c. a dog who visits his girlfriend.

2. People were amazed when they heard about Shiro because

   a. dogs don't usually fall in love.

   b. swimming from Aka to Zamami is very difficult.

   c. "Shiro" is an unusual name for a dog.

◆ **UNDERSTANDING CAUSE AND EFFECT**

Find the best way to complete each sentence. Write the letter of the answer on the line.

1. Mr. and Mrs. Nakamura were worried ___c___

2. Shiro was always wet when he came back _____

3. Mr. Nakamura followed Shiro _____

4. Shiro swam to Zamami _____

5. Three thousand people went to Zamami _____

   a. because his girlfriend lived there.

   b. because he was curious.

   c. because their dog was missing.

   d. because he swam in the ocean.

   e. because they wanted to see Shiro.

◆ **REVIEWING THE STORY**

Write the missing words. Then read the story again and check your answers.

Mr. Nakamura was curious about his dog, Shiro. Shiro often
____*disappeared*____ in the morning and _____ back late at
1.   **2.**
night. He _____ always wet when he came back.
          3.

One morning Mr. Nakamura _____ Shiro. Shiro walked to
                                  4.
the beach, ran into the water, and began to _____. He swam
                                                   5.
to Zamami, a Japanese island. Marilyn lived on Zamami. Marilyn was

Shiro's _____.
              6.

4   Unit 1

People were amazed when they heard _____ Shiro. The
_____ from Aka to Zamami is two and a half miles, and the
8.
ocean between the islands is very _____.
9.

Shiro became _____. Many people went to Zamami because
10.
they wanted to see Shiro, the dog who was in _____.
11.

4. DISCUSSION/WRITING

A. Shiro is the Nakamuras' pet. Interview a classmate who has a pet. Ask your classmate the questions below. Listen carefully and write your classmate's answers. Then tell the class what you learned about your classmate's pet.

1. What kind of pet do you have?

   _____

2. What is your pet's name?

   _____

3. How old is your pet?

   _____

4. Is your pet smart like Shiro?

   _____

5. Does your pet do anything unusual?

   _____

6. What do you like to do with your pet?

   _____

7. Do you want more pets?

   _____

B. Use your classmate's answers to write a paragraph on your own paper. Here is what one student wrote.

Irma has a pet goldfish. His name is Tiger, and he is about one year old. Irma named her fish Tiger because he has stripes like a tiger. Tiger is not smart like Shiro. Tiger doesn't do anything unusual. He just swims around in his goldfish bowl. Maybe Irma will buy another goldfish. Then Tiger will have a friend.

UNIT 2

1. PRE-READING

Look at the picture.

▸ What is the woman holding? Why do you think she is holding them?

▸ What is the man doing?

Read the title of the story. Look at the picture again.

▸ What do you think this story is about?

▸ Can you guess what happens?

Surprise! It's Your Wedding!

"Good night, John."

"Good night, Lynn."

Lynn Millington kissed her boyfriend good night. He walked to his car and drove away. Lynn walked into her house. It was midnight. Her parents were sleeping, and the house was quiet. Lynn sat down on the sofa. She had a problem, and she needed some time to think.

Lynn's boyfriend was John Biggin. John loved Lynn, and Lynn loved John. They were very happy together. What was the problem? Lynn wanted to get married. John wanted to get married, too, but he was afraid.

Sometimes Lynn and John talked about getting married. "Let's get married in June," Lynn said. "June is a beautiful month for a wedding."

"June?" John asked. "This June? Let's not get married in June. Let's wait a little longer."

Lynn waited . . . and waited. She was very patient. She was patient, but she wanted to get married. Lynn's parents wanted her to get married, too; they liked John. John's parents also wanted them to get married because they liked Lynn. Suddenly Lynn had an idea. "John's parents will help me!" she thought.

The next morning, Lynn called John's parents. "I need your help," Lynn told them. "John wants to get married, but he's afraid. Let's plan a wedding for John and me. It will be this Saturday. Invite your family. But don't tell John about the wedding."

Next, Lynn called Bob Raper. Bob was John's best friend. "I need your help," Lynn told Bob. "Tell John that you're getting married this Saturday. Invite him to your wedding."

Bob wasn't really getting married on Saturday. It was a trick. John and Lynn were getting married on Saturday, but John didn't know it.

On Saturday morning, John put on his best suit. Then he drove to the courthouse in Bridlington, England. He walked into the courthouse and looked around. He saw his friend Bob. He saw his girlfriend, Lynn. Then he saw his parents, relatives, and friends. He saw Lynn's family and friends. Suddenly John understood. This was not Bob's wedding! This was John's wedding! John began to shake, but he didn't run away. Twenty minutes later, John and Lynn were husband and wife.

After the wedding, a photographer took pictures of John and Lynn. In one picture, John is pretending to punch Lynn. He is pretending that he is angry. John is not really angry; he is smiling. Lynn, of course, is smiling, too.

2. VOCABULARY

Complete the sentences with the words below.

courthouse	~~patient~~	punch	trick	wedding

1. Lynn waited and waited. She was very _____*patient*_____.

2. John's best friend, Bob, told him, "I'm getting married on Saturday." That wasn't true; Bob wasn't really getting married. It was a _____.

3. John and Lynn live in England. In England people get married at a church or at a _____.

4. Lynn and Bob got married. After the _____, a photographer took pictures.

5. In the picture on page 6, Bob is pretending to _____ Lynn.

3. COMPREHENSION

◆ **UNDERSTANDING THE MAIN IDEA**

Circle the letter of the best answer.

1. What was Lynn's problem?

   a. John's parents didn't like her.

   b. Lynn loved John's best friend.

   c. John was afraid to get married.

2. John and Lynn's wedding was unusual because

   a. Lynn didn't wear a white dress.

   b. John didn't know about the wedding.

   c. the wedding was at a courthouse.

◆ **UNDERSTANDING CONNECTIONS**

Find the best way to complete each sentence. Write the letter of the answer on the line.

1. John wanted to get married, but ___*b*___

2. Lynn was patient, but _____

3. Lynn told John's parents, "Invite your family to the wedding, but _____

4. When John understood that it was his wedding, he began to shake, but _____

   a. don't tell John."

   b. he was afraid.

   c. he didn't run away.

   d. she wanted to get married.

◆ **REMEMBERING DETAILS**

One word in each sentence is not correct. Find the word and cross it out. Write the correct word.

1. John loved Lynn and wanted to get married, but he was ~~angry~~. *afraid*

2. Lynn told John's brothers, "I need your help."

3. "Let's plan a party for John and me," Lynn told John's parents.

4. Next, Lynn called Bob Raper, who was John's boss.

5. She told him, "Tell John that you're getting married this Monday, and invite him to the wedding."

6. Bob wasn't really getting married; it was a problem.

7. On Saturday morning, John put on his best suit and drove to the library in Bridlington, England.

8. At the courthouse, he called Lynn, his friends, and his relatives.

9. Suddenly he understood: This was Bob's wedding!

10. Twenty minutes later, John and Lynn were boyfriend and wife.

4. DISCUSSION

Read the sentences and circle *YES* or *NO*. Then read the sentences and your answers to a partner. Explain your answers.

1. I think John is happy that he married Lynn.   **YES**   **NO**

2. Lynn tricked John. I think that was a good idea.   **YES**   **NO**

3. In the picture, John is wearing a suit. Lynn is wearing a dress, and she has flowers in her hair. In my native country, people sometimes dress like this for their wedding.   **YES**   **NO**

4. John is 24 years old. That is a good age for a man to get married.   **YES**   **NO**

5. I am (I was) afraid to get married.   **YES**   **NO**

5. WRITING

Is it better to be married or single? Fill in the chart below. Then discuss your answers with your classmates.

It is better to be married. Why?	It is better to be single. Why?
1. _____ _____	1. _____ _____
2. _____ _____	2. _____ _____
3. _____ _____	3. _____ _____

UNIT 3

1. PRE-READING

Look at the picture.

▶ How old is the man?

▶ Where does he live?

▶ How does he feel?

Read the title of the story. Look at the picture again.

▶ What do you think the man's bad news was?

▶ What do you think his good news was?

▶ What do you think this story is about?

▶ Can you guess what happens?

Bad News, Good News

John Brandrick had a terrible pain in his stomach, so he went to his doctor. The doctor sent him to the hospital for tests and then told him the bad news. "Mr. Brandrick, you are a very sick man," the doctor said. "You have only six months to live."

"Isn't there anything you can do?" John asked the doctor. "Medicine? Surgery?"

"I'm sorry," the doctor answered. "There's nothing we can do. Enjoy the time you have left. I'm very, very sorry."

John was 62 years old. He was divorced and had two grown children. He told his children the bad news. Then he told Sally, his girlfriend. "Let's not be sad," he told them. "The doctor told me, 'Enjoy the time you have left.' That's what we're going to do. We're going to enjoy every minute of the rest of my life."

The next day, John quit his job. He had $23,000 in savings, and he decided to spend it. John and Sally lived on the coast of England, in a beautiful area where tourists often visit. John and Sally took short trips along the coast and ate at all the best restaurants. John bought expensive gifts for his family and friends.

All spring and summer, John spent his money. When fall came, he began thinking about his death. "What will my family do with all my things after I die?" he wondered. "I'll sell my things now so my family won't have to."

John sold most of his furniture. Then he sold his car. "I won't need my winter clothes," he thought, "because I won't be alive this winter." He gave all his winter clothes away. He kept only a black suit, a white shirt, and a red tie. "Bury me in that suit," he told Sally.

Fall came and went. Winter came and went. Spring came again, and John was still alive. He went back to his doctor.

"How's the stomach pain?" the doctor asked.

"It's gone," John said.

The doctor sent John to the hospital for tests and then told him the good news. "You are in perfect health," the doctor said.

"So I'm not going to die soon?" John asked.

"No," the doctor said. "I think you're fine."

"But what about the tests I had at the hospital a year ago?" John asked.

"I don't know," the doctor said. "Maybe there was a mistake."

John told Sally and his children the good news, and they had a big celebration. But later John thought, "I'm going to live. But *how* am I going to live with no job, no furniture, no car, no warm clothes, and no money?"

John wants the hospital to pay him for its mistake. So he is going to court. He wants the hospital to give him money for new furniture, a new car, and new clothes. He also wants the hospital to put $23,000 in his savings account. A judge will decide if the hospital has to give John money. John is hoping the judge will give him more good news.

2. VOCABULARY

Which words have the same meaning as the words in *italics*? Write the letter of the answer on the line.

___e___ **1.** John had two *adult* children.

_____ **2.** "Enjoy the *rest of your life*," the doctor said.

_____ **3.** "*I don't want us to* be sad," John told his family.

_____ **4.** John had $23,000 in *his bank account*.

_____ **5.** John and his family had a *party*.

a. Let's not

b. celebration

c. time you have left

d. savings

e. grown

3. COMPREHENSION

◆ **UNDERSTANDING THE MAIN IDEAS**

There are two correct ways to complete each sentence. Circle the letters of the *two* correct answers.

1. John's doctor told him,
   - **a.** "You are a very sick man."
   - **b.** "You have a bad heart."
   - **c.** "You have only six months to live."

2. When John asked his doctor, "Isn't there anything you can do?" the doctor answered,
   - **a.** "We can try surgery."
   - **b.** "There's nothing we can do."
   - **c.** "I'm very, very sorry."

3. John wanted to enjoy the time he had left, so he
   - **a.** quit his job.
   - **b.** married his girlfriend, Sally.
   - **c.** spent his savings.

4. John decided to sell
   - **a.** most of his furniture.
   - **b.** his car.
   - **c.** his house.

5. When John returned to his doctor one year later, the doctor told him,
   - **a.** "You are in perfect health."
   - **b.** "Maybe the hospital made a mistake."
   - **c.** "You should go to court."

6. John wants the hospital to
   - **a.** give money to Sally and his children.
   - **b.** give him money for new furniture, a new car, and new clothes.
   - **c.** give him $23,000 for his savings account.

◆ **FINDING INFORMATION**

Read each question. Find the answer in the paragraphs below and on the next page and circle it. Write the number of the question above the answer.

1. How old was John?
2. How many children did he have?
3. What was his girlfriend's name?
4. When did John quit his job?
5. How much money did John have in savings?
6. Where did John and Sally live?
7. Where did they eat?
8. What did John buy?

John was 62 years old. He was divorced and had two grown children. He told his children the bad news. Then he told Sally, his girlfriend. "Let's not be sad," he told them. "Let's enjoy the time I have left."

The next day, John quit his job. He had $23,000 in savings, and he decided to spend it. John and Sally lived on the coast of England, in a beautiful area where tourists often visit. John and Sally took short trips along the coast and ate at all the best restaurants. John bought expensive gifts for his family and friends.

◆ **UNDERSTANDING A SUMMARY**

Imagine this: You want to tell the story "Bad News, Good News" to a friend. You want to tell the story quickly, in only four sentences. Which four sentences tell the story best? Check (✓) the answer.

☐ **1.** John Brandrick had terrible stomach pains, so he went to his doctor. After John had some tests at the hospital, his doctor told him he had only six months to live. John has two grown children and a girlfriend named Sally. He wanted to enjoy the rest of his life with Sally and his children, so he quit his job and spent all his savings.

☐ **2.** John Brandrick's doctor sent him to the hospital for tests and then told him he was going to die. So John quit his job, spent his savings, sold his car and most of his furniture, and gave away his winter clothes. But the tests were wrong; John is not going to die. John wants the hospital to pay him for its mistake.

4. DISCUSSION/WRITING

A. John wants the hospital to pay him for its mistake. Do you think the hospital should pay him?

Check (✓) your answer. Then complete the sentence you checked. Explain your answer in a small group.

Should the hospital pay John?

☐ No, I don't think the hospital should pay John because _____

_____.

☐ Yes, I think the hospital should pay John $ _____ because

_____.

B. John told Sally and his children, "We're going to enjoy every minute of the rest of my life." What do you enjoy in *your* life?

Make a list of some things you enjoy. They can be big things (for example, your children or good health), or they can be small things (for example, your morning cup of tea or your new shoes). Write your list on the lines below. Then share your list with a partner.

_____   _____

_____   _____

UNIT 4

1. PRE-READING

Look at the picture.

▶ Where do you think these people are from?

▶ How old do you think this photo is?

▶ What is unusual about the two men?

Read the title of the story. Look at the picture again.

▶ What do you think this story is about?

▶ Can you guess what happens?

The Twins of Siam

A young mother was lying on a bed. She had just given birth to twin boys. She was tired but happy. A woman was helping her. Suddenly the woman screamed. "What's the matter?" the mother cried. She lifted her head and looked at her babies. The babies were joined at their chests. She could not separate them.

That happened in Siam—now called Thailand—in 1811. The mother named her babies Chang and Eng. Chang and Eng grew up and became the famous Siamese twins.

People came from all over Siam to stare at the twins. One day, when the twins were 18, an American saw them. He thought, "I can make money with the twins." He asked Chang and Eng, "Will you come with me to the United States?" Chang and Eng wanted to go to the United States, so they went with the man. They never saw Siam or their family again.

Chang and Eng traveled with the American for ten years. Later they traveled alone. People paid to see them and ask them questions about their lives. Finally, the twins got tired of traveling. They got tired of answering questions. They decided to live quietly in North Carolina.

Soon after they moved to North Carolina, the twins met two sisters. The sisters' names were Adelaide and Sarah. The twins fell in love with the sisters. Chang married Adelaide, and Eng married Sarah. The marriages were very unusual. Adelaide and Sarah lived in separate houses. The twins lived in one house for four days. Then they went to the other house for four days. The marriages were unusual, but they were long and happy. Chang and Adelaide had ten children, and Eng and Sarah had eleven children.

The twins were happy with Adelaide and Sarah, but they were not always happy with each other. Sometimes they argued, and they didn't talk to each other. They asked doctor after doctor, "Please separate us." Every doctor said, "I can't separate you. The operation is too dangerous." So, the twins stayed joined together.

One night, when the twins were 63, Eng suddenly woke up. He looked at Chang, who was lying beside him. Chang was not breathing. Eng screamed for help, and one of his sons came.

"Uncle Chang is dead," the young man said.

"Then I am going to die, too," Eng said, and he began to cry. Two hours later, Eng was dead.

For 63 years, the twins of Siam lived together as one. In the end, they also died as one.

2. VOCABULARY

Complete the sentences with the words below.

argued	got tired	~~joined~~	stare

1. The twins were together, and their mother couldn't separate them. They were ___*joined*___ at their chests.

2. People looked at Chang and Eng because the twins were unusual. People came from all over Siam to _____ at them.

3. After traveling for many years, the twins didn't want to travel anymore. They _____ of it.

4. Sometimes the twins spoke in angry voices. They _____ because they were not happy with each other.

3. COMPREHENSION

◆ **UNDERSTANDING THE MAIN IDEA**

Circle the letter of the best answer.

1. This story is about
   a. dangerous operations.
   b. unusual marriages.
   c. Siamese twin brothers.

2. The twins talked to many doctors because
   a. the twins were often sick.
   b. they wanted the doctors to separate them.
   c. the doctors wanted to study the twins.

◆ **REMEMBERING DETAILS**

One word in each sentence is not correct. Find the incorrect word and cross it out. Write the correct word.

1. The story happened in Siam—now called ~~China~~ *Thailand* —in 1811.

2. Chang and Eng grew up and became the famous Siamese doctors.

3. People came from all over Siam to laugh at the twins.

4. An Australian asked Chang and Eng to come with him to the United States.

5. Chang and Eng traveled with the American for ten days.

6. After they moved to North Carolina, the twins met two cousins.

7. The marriages were unusual, but they were long and unhappy.

8. Every doctor said, "I can separate you because the operation is too dangerous."

◆ **UNDERSTANDING REASONS**

Find the best way to complete each sentence. Write the letter of the answer on the line.

1. The young mother lifted her head ___e___

2. Chang and Eng went to the United States _____

3. People paid _____

4. The twins moved to North Carolina _____

5. The twins went to doctor after doctor _____

   a. to live quietly.

   b. to ask the twins questions.

   c. to ask about an operation.

   d. to travel with the American.

   e. to look at her babies.

4. DISCUSSION

The twins of Siam were famous. People paid to see them and ask them questions about their lives.

Play the game "Twenty Questions" with your classmates. Think of a famous person, living or dead. Tell your teacher who you are thinking of, but don't tell your classmates. Then sit in front of the class. Your classmates will ask you questions, and you will answer only "yes" or "no." Can your classmates guess who you are in fewer than 20 questions? Here are some sample questions.

- ▸ Are you a woman?
- ▸ Are you alive?
- ▸ Are you an actor?
- ▸ Are you rich?
- ▸ Did you live a long time ago?

- ▸ Are you a political leader?
- ▸ Are you French?
- ▸ Are you an athlete?
- ▸ Are you a singer?
- ▸ Are you handsome?

5. WRITING

The twins married two sisters. Their marriages were happy. Not all marriages are happy every day.

Look at this picture of a husband and wife. Why is the husband angry? What is he saying? Write it.

Look at the next picture. Why is the wife angry? What is she saying? Write it.

What did you write? Tell your classmates.

UNIT
5

1. PRE-READING

Look at the picture.

▶ Why do you think the women are smiling?

▶ How old do you think the babies are?

Read the title of the story. Look at the picture again.

▶ What do you think this story is about?

▶ Can you guess what happens?

The Baby Exchange

Selma Scarausi looked at her baby daughter and smiled. The baby smiled back. Selma began to cry. "I love my baby very much," Selma thought. "But is she really my baby?"

Selma's baby was born at a hospital in São Paulo, Brazil. A few days later, Selma and the baby came home from the hospital. Friends and relatives were surprised when they saw the baby. The baby didn't look like her parents. The baby had dark skin and curly hair, but Selma and her husband had light skin and straight hair. "Babies change," everyone thought. "She will look like her parents when she is older."

But the baby didn't change. When she was nine months old, she still looked very different from her parents. Selma and her husband Paulo took the baby back to the hospital. "Are you sure this is our baby?" they asked the hospital director.

"Of course she is your baby," the director said. "Immediately after the babies are born, we give them bracelets with numbers. Your baby was number 51. You left the hospital with baby 51. A mistake is impossible."

"A mistake *is* possible," Selma and Paulo thought. "We have another family's baby. And somewhere another family has our baby. But São Paulo is a city of seven million people. How can we find our baby?"

Selma and Paulo went to the hospital again. A nurse at the hospital told Paulo, "I remember another couple. Their baby didn't look like them. The parents had dark skin, but the baby had light skin. The father had very curly hair, but the baby had straight hair." The nurse gave Paulo the couple's address.

The next day, Selma took her baby to the couple's house. She knocked, and a woman opened the door. The woman took one look at Selma's baby and fainted. Selma helped her into the house. There, in the living room, was a nine-month-old baby. Selma knew that the baby was hers.

Selma and Paulo's baby was living with Maria and Luiz Souza. The Souzas also had wondered about their baby because she looked so different from them. When Maria Souza saw the baby in Selma's arms, she, too, knew the baby was hers.

The hospital made a mistake. Both babies were born at the hospital on the same day. The hospital gave both babies the number 51.

During the next weeks, the two families prepared to exchange babies. First, they exchanged information about the babies' habits. Then they exchanged toys and clothes. Finally, with smiles and tears, they exchanged babies.

2. VOCABULARY

Which picture or words have the same meaning as the words in *italics*? Circle the letter of the answer.

1. The hospital gave the babies *bracelets* with numbers.

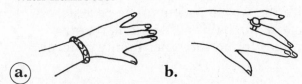

   a.   **b.**

2. Maria Souza took one look at Selma's baby and *fainted*.

   a. left the house with the baby

   b. fell to the floor and didn't move

3. The two families exchanged information about the babies' *habits*.

   a. things people do every day

   b. places people like to go

4. Finally, with smiles and *tears*, they exchanged babies.

   a. water that comes from people's eyes when they cry

   b. gifts that people give to babies

3. COMPREHENSION

◆ **UNDERSTANDING THE MAIN IDEA**

Circle the letter of the best answer.

1. The story is about
   a. the city of São Paulo, Brazil.
   b. two couples who got the wrong babies.
   c. babies' habits, toys, and clothes.

2. Selma and Paulo thought, "We have the wrong baby" because
   a. hospitals sometimes make mistakes.
   b. they wanted a son, not a daughter.
   c. their baby didn't look like them.

◆ **UNDERSTANDING CAUSE AND EFFECT**

Find the best way to complete each sentence. Write the letter of the answer on the line.

1. Friends and relatives were surprised ___*e*___

2. Selma and Paulo went back to the hospital _____

3. The hospital director said that a mistake was impossible _____

4. It was difficult for Selma and Paulo to find their baby _____

5. Maria Souza fainted _____

a. because São Paulo is a big city.

b. because she knew that the baby in Selma's arms was her baby.

c. because they thought they had the wrong baby.

d. because the hospital gave each baby a number.

e. because the baby didn't look like her parents.

◆ **UNDERSTANDING A SUMMARY**

Imagine this: You want to tell the story "The Baby Exchange" to a friend. You want to tell the story quickly, in only four sentences. Which four sentences tell the story best? Check (✓) the answer.

☐ 1. There was a mistake at a hospital in Brazil. Two babies were born on the same day and went home with the wrong parents. The parents wondered about their babies because the babies didn't look them. Nine months later, one of the families found the other family, and the two families exchanged babies.

☐ 2. A Brazilian woman had a baby at a hospital in São Paulo. She wondered about her baby because the baby didn't look like her or her husband. When the baby was nine months old, the woman and her husband took their baby to the hospital. They asked the hospital director, "Are you sure this is our baby?"

4. DISCUSSION/WRITING

A. Before the families exchanged babies, they exchanged information about the babies' habits. What habits do the people in your class have? Find out.

First, count off (1, 2, 3, 4 . . .) until everyone in the class has a number. Write your number on a piece of paper and tape it to your shirt. Now look for your number in the list below. Look at the question next to your number. That is *your* question.

1. Do you sleep in the afternoon?
2. Do you sing in the shower?
3. Do you exercise?
4. Do you bite your nails?
5. Do you come to class late?
6. Do you walk fast?
7. Do you sleep with two pillows?
8. Do you go to bed after midnight?
9. Do you read before you go to sleep?
10. Do you drink coffee in the morning?
11. Do you spend a lot of money on phone calls?
12. Do you make your bed every day?
13. Do you bring a notebook to English class?
14. Do you sing when you drive a car?
15. Do you pick up coins you find on the street?
16. Do you listen to music when you study?
17. Do you check your e-mail when you get up in the morning?

Write your question at the top of a piece of paper. Write numbers under the question, as many numbers as there are people in your class. Then walk around the room. Ask people your question. Write each person's answer next to his or her number. Write your own answer next to your number, too. For example:

> Do you sleep in the afternoon?
>
> 1. Yes.
> 2. No, never.
> 3. Sometimes, if I am really tired.

After you ask everyone your question and write their answers, report back to the class. Tell the class what you learned. For example:

"Only four people always sleep in the afternoon. Two people sometimes sleep in the afternoon. The rest of the class never sleeps in the afternoon."

B. Do your family and friends have any habits that you don't like? Write about them on your own paper. For example:

▸ When we go somewhere, my mother always loses something.
▸ My friend eats bananas like a monkey.

UNIT 6

1. PRE-READING

Look at the picture.

▸ What time of day is it?

▸ Why isn't anyone sleeping in this bed?

Read the title of the story. Look at the picture again.

▸ What do you think this story is about?

▸ Can you guess what happens?

The Ghost

One night at 2 A.M., Alfred Mansbridge heard something and woke up. He sat up in bed and listened. Someone was speaking in a quiet voice. It sounded like a child . . . or maybe a ghost.

Alfred was a 69-year-old widower, and he lived alone. He looked around his bedroom. There was nobody there.

"Maybe I was dreaming," Alfred thought. He went back to sleep.

The next night at 2 A.M., Alfred heard the quiet voice again. He sat up in bed and listened carefully. "Come and catch me," the voice said. It repeated the sentence five times. Then it was silent. That night Alfred lay awake for a long time.

For the next three months, Alfred heard the quiet voice every night at 2 A.M. "Come and catch me," it repeated for 15 seconds. Sometimes Alfred got up and searched his apartment, but he never found anyone or anything. He began to have trouble sleeping. Some nights he didn't sleep at all.

One day Alfred's daughter and seven-year-old grandson came to visit. "Dad, are you okay?" his daughter asked. "You look tired."

"I *am* tired," Alfred told her. "Every night at 2 A.M., a quiet voice wakes me up. It says, 'Come and catch me.' I'm having trouble sleeping."

"I'm worried about you," his daughter said. "I think you're alone too much."

"My daughter thinks I'm crazy," Alfred thought. "But I'm not crazy; the voice is real! It's not a ghost—I don't believe in ghosts. So who is speaking to me every night? This is a real mystery, and I'm going to solve it."

The next day, Alfred bought a tape recorder. At 2 A.M., he recorded the quiet voice. Then he played the recording for his daughter. She immediately called the police. "Someone—or something—is in my father's apartment!" she told the police.

That night two police officers came to Alfred's apartment. One police officer sat in the kitchen, and the other sat in the living room. Alfred was in the bedroom. At 2 A.M., they all heard the quiet voice. "Come and catch me," it said.

"It's in here!" the police officer in the living room shouted. "It's coming from the bookcase!"

Alfred and the two police officers looked at the bookcase. At first, they saw only books. Then they spotted a plastic children's watch on a low shelf in the bookcase. It was a Spider-Man watch, and in a quiet voice, it repeated a line from the movie *Spider-Man*: "Come and catch me." It repeated the line five times. Then it was silent. Alfred picked up the watch and looked at it. The alarm on the watch was set for 2 A.M.

"This is my grandson's watch," Alfred explained to the police officers. "He loved the movie *Spider-Man*, so my daughter bought him this watch a few months ago. I guess he left it here."

The next day, Alfred returned the watch to his grandson. "My Spider-Man watch!" his grandson said. "I was looking for that!"

That night Alfred slept well. The voice was gone.

2. VOCABULARY

Complete the sentences with the words below.

~~ghost~~	searched	spotted	widower

1. Nobody could see the person with the quiet voice. Maybe it was a _____*ghost*_____.

2. Alfred's wife died a few years ago. He is a _____.

3. Alfred looked everywhere. He _____ every room in his apartment.

4. Alfred and the police officers looked at the bookcase but didn't see anything unusual.

   Then they _____ the watch on a low shelf.

3. COMPREHENSION

◆ **UNDERSTANDING A SUMMARY**

A. Complete the sentences. Write the answers on the lines.

1. When Alfred's _____*daughter*_____ heard the recording, she called the

   _____ .

2. Every _____ at 2 A.M., Alfred Mansbridge heard a

   _____ voice.

3. In a bookcase in the _____ room, Alfred and the police

   officers found a children's _____ .

4. The quiet voice was _____ after Alfred returned the watch to

   his _____ .

5. Alfred wanted to record the voice, so he went to a store and

   _____ a _____ recorder.

B. On your own paper, copy the sentences above in the correct order to make a summary of the story. Write your summary in a paragraph.

Every night at 2 A.M., Alfred Mansbridge heard a quiet voice.

◆ **UNDERSTANDING QUOTATIONS**

Who said it? Write the letter of the answer on the line.

___*c*___ 1. "Come and catch me."   **a.** a police officer

_____ 2. "I *am* tired."   **b.** Alfred's grandson

_____ 3. "I think you're alone too much." **c.** the quiet voice

_____ 4. "It's coming from the bookcase!" **d.** Alfred

_____ 5. "I was looking for that!"   **e.** Alfred's daughter

◆ **REMEMBERING DETAILS**

1. Which sentences describe Alfred Mansbridge? Check (✓) six answers. (The first one is done for you.)

☑ He is 69 years old.   ☐ He has a daughter.

☐ He is a widower.   ☐ He had trouble sleeping.

☐ He lives in a big house.   ☐ He is a police officer.

☐ He lives alone.   ☐ He is a grandfather.

2. Which sentences describe the quiet voice? Check (✓) six answers.

☐ It sounded like a ghost or a child.

☐ Alfred heard it only in the kitchen.

☐ Alfred heard it every night for 15 seconds.

☐ It said, "Come and catch me."

☐ It repeated the sentence five times.

☐ Alfred's neighbors heard it, too.

☐ It woke Alfred up.

☐ It came from a watch.

4. DISCUSSION/WRITING

A. Alfred had trouble sleeping. Some nights he didn't sleep at all. What about you? How many hours do you sleep at night?

Line up at the front of the room. The person who sleeps the fewest hours will stand at the beginning of the line. The person who sleeps the most hours will stand at the end of the line. The people in between will stand in order of the number of hours they sleep. If you don't get enough sleep, tell the class why you don't.

B. What can you do to get a good night's sleep? Write your ideas on the lines below. Then share your ideas with the class. For example:

Don't watch a scary movie before you go to bed.

_____

_____

_____

1. PRE-READING

Look at the picture.

▸ What is the man doing?

Read the title of the story. Look at the picture again.

▸ What do you think this story is about?

▸ What do you think the man wants to do?

Why Can't They Quit?

The man in the picture is Ali. Ali is from Saudi Arabia, but he is living in the United States. Ali will stay in the United States for one year. During the year, Ali wants to do two things. First, he wants to learn English. Second, he wants to quit smoking.

Ali has smoked for nine years. He smokes a pack of cigarettes every day. Ali says, "I tried to quit smoking in Saudi Arabia, but it was impossible. My brothers smoke. All my friends smoke. At parties and at meetings, almost all the men smoke. Here in the United States, not as many people smoke. It will be easier to quit here."

Many smokers are like Ali: They want to quit smoking. They know that smoking is bad for their health. They know it can cause cancer and heart disease. But it is difficult for them to stop smoking because cigarettes have a drug in them. The drug is *nicotine*. People who smoke a lot need nicotine.

The first few times a person smokes, the smoker usually feels terrible. The nicotine makes the person sick. In a few days, the smoker's body gets used to the nicotine, and the smoker feels fine.

Later, the smoker needs nicotine to feel fine. Without it, the smoker feels terrible. The smoker is addicted to nicotine.

What happens when people quit smoking? What happens when smokers don't have nicotine? People who quit smoking are often depressed and nervous for weeks. Some people eat instead of smoking, so they gain weight.

Doctors sometimes give special chewing gum to people who want to quit smoking. The chewing gum has a little nicotine in it. When smokers need nicotine, they don't smoke cigarettes. They chew the gum instead. Each day the smokers try to chew the gum less often. With the gum, people can quit smoking and then gradually give up nicotine.

It is very difficult to quit smoking, and many people who quit will smoke again. At a party or maybe at work, they will decide to smoke "just one" cigarette. Then they will smoke another cigarette, and another. Soon they are smokers again. Maybe there is only one easy way to quit smoking: Never start.

2. VOCABULARY

Complete the sentences with the words below.

causes	gets used to	pack	~~quit~~

1. Ali tried to stop smoking in Saudi Arabia, but it was impossible. He hopes it will be easier to _____quit_____ smoking in the United States.

2. There are 20 cigarettes in a _____.

3. Sometimes people who smoke get cancer or a bad heart because smoking _____ these diseases.

4. When a smoker smokes for the first time, the nicotine makes the smoker sick. In a few days, the smoker feels fine because the smoker's body _____ the nicotine.

3. COMPREHENSION

◆ **UNDERSTANDING THE MAIN IDEA**

Circle the letter of the best answer.

1. It is difficult to quit smoking because
   a. people don't know it is bad for their health.
   b. many people who quit will smoke again.
   c. smokers are addicted to nicotine.

2. Nicotine is
   a. a kind of chewing gum.
   b. a drug in cigarettes.
   c. a popular food in Saudi Arabia.

◆ **FINDING MORE INFORMATION**

Read each sentence on the left. Which sentence on the right gives you more information? Write the letter of the answer on the line.

__c__ 1. Ali wants to do two things.	**a.** It can cause cancer and heart disease.
_____ 2. Ali smokes.	
_____ 3. Smoking is bad for the smoker's health.	**b.** It has a little nicotine in it, so people chew the gum instead of smoking.
_____ 4. There is a special chewing gum for people who want to quit smoking.	**c.** He wants to learn English, and he wants to quit smoking.
	d. He smokes a pack of cigarettes every day.

◆ **REVIEWING THE STORY**

Write the missing words. Then read the story again and check your answers.

It is difficult to quit smoking because smokers are _____*addicted*_____ to
1.
nicotine. Nicotine is a _____ that is in cigarettes.
2.

People who quit _____ are often depressed and nervous. Some
3.
people gain _____ because they eat sweets instead of smoking.
4.

People who want to quit smoking sometimes chew a special

_____. The gum has a _____ nicotine in it. When
5. **6.**
smokers need nicotine, they _____ the gum.
7.

It is very difficult to _____ smoking, and many people who
8.
quit will _____ again. Maybe there is only one easy
9.
_____ to quit smoking: Never start.
10.

4. DISCUSSION

Read the sentences and circle *YES* or *NO*. Then read the sentences and your answers to a partner. Explain your answers.

1. A lot of men in my native country smoke.   YES   NO

2. A lot of women in my native country smoke.   YES   NO

3. A lot of children in my native country smoke.   YES   NO

4. In my native country, smoking is not allowed in
   some places.   YES   NO

5. I smoke a little.   YES   NO

6. I smoke a lot.   YES   NO

7. I began smoking when I was young.   YES   NO

8. I used to smoke, but I quit.   YES   NO

9. I have never smoked a cigarette.   YES   NO

10. I think cigarette smoke smells good.   YES   NO

5. WRITING

Many people think smoking is a bad habit. There are other bad habits. Some people, for example, drink too much coffee. Some people watch too much TV.

What are your bad habits—habits you want to stop? What are your good habits—habits you want to keep? Make two lists and share your lists with a partner.

MY BAD HABITS

1. _____

2. _____

MY GOOD HABITS

1. _____

2. _____

UNIT 8

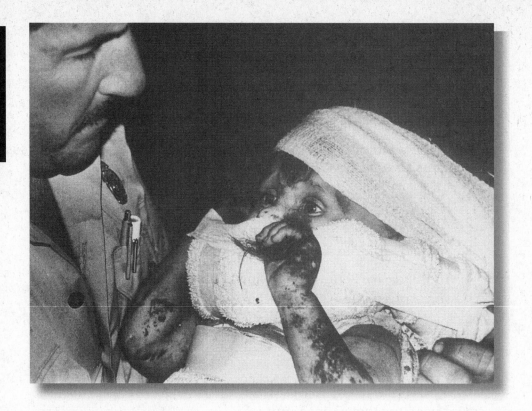

1. PRE-READING

Look at the picture.

▸ How old is the little girl?

▸ How do you think she feels?

▸ What does she have around her head?

▸ Who is holding the little girl?

Read the title of the story. Look at the picture again.

▸ What do you think this story is about?

▸ Can you guess what happens?

Everybody's Baby

At a daycare center in Texas, children were playing outside. One of the children was Jessica McClure. She was 18 months old. Jessica's mother, who worked at the daycare center, was watching the children. Suddenly Jessica fell and disappeared. Jessica's mother screamed and ran to her.

A well was in the yard of the daycare center. The well was only eight inches across, and a rock always covered it. But children had moved the rock. When Jessica fell, she fell right into the well.

Jessica's mother reached inside the well, but she couldn't feel Jessica. She ran to a phone and dialed 911 for help.

Men from the fire department arrived. They discovered that Jessica was about 20 feet[1] down in the well. For the next hour, the men talked and planned Jessica's rescue. Then they told Jessica's parents their plan.

"We can't go down into the well," they said. "It's too narrow. So, we're going to drill a hole next to the well. We'll drill down about 20 feet. Then we'll drill a tunnel across to Jessica. When we reach her, we'll bring her through the tunnel. Then we'll bring her up through our hole."

The men began to drill the hole on a Wednesday morning. "We'll reach Jessica in a few hours," they thought. The men were wrong. They had to drill through solid rock. Two days later, on Friday morning, they were still drilling. And Jessica McClure was still in the well.

During her days in the well, Jessica sometimes called for her mother. Sometimes she slept, sometimes she cried, and sometimes she sang.

All over the world, people waited for news of Jessica. They read about her in newspapers and watched her rescue on TV. Everyone worried about the little girl in the well.

At 8 P.M. on Friday, the men finally reached Jessica and brought her up from the well. Then paramedics rushed her to the hospital. Jessica was dirty, hungry, thirsty, and tired. Her foot and forehead were badly injured. But Jessica was alive. A doctor at the hospital said, "Jessica is lucky she's very young. She's not going to remember this very well."

Jessica McClure is in her 20s now. She is happy and healthy. The doctor who said, "She's not going to remember this very well" was right: Jessica doesn't remember the 58 hours she was in the well. Although Jessica doesn't remember her days in the well, her rescuers and many other people around the world will not forget them. They will always remember the little girl who sang and cried in the well. For three days in 1987, she was everybody's baby.

[1] 6 meters

2. VOCABULARY

Complete the sentences with the words below.

~~daycare center~~	dialed	drill	injured	narrow

1. Jessica's mother took care of small children. She worked at a ___daycare center___.

2. The well was only eight inches across. It was _____.

3. After Jessica fell into the well, her mother ran to the phone and _____ 911.

4. The men used machines to _____ a hole next to the well.

5. Paramedics rushed Jessica to the hospital. Her foot and forehead were badly

_____.

3. COMPREHENSION

◆ **UNDERSTANDING THE MAIN IDEA**

Circle the letter of the best answer.

1. This story is about

   a. daycare centers in Texas.

   b. the rescue of a little girl.

   c. drilling wells.

2. The story has a happy ending because

   a. Jessica was very young.

   b. Jessica was in the well only two days.

   c. the men rescued Jessica.

◆ **UNDERSTANDING TIME RELATIONSHIPS**

Find the best way to complete each sentence. Write the letter of the answer on the line.

1. When Jessica fell, __*d*__

2. When Jessica's mother reached inside the well, _____

3. When the men from the fire department arrived, _____

4. When Jessica was in the well, _____

5. When the rescuers reached Jessica, _____

   a. she slept, cried, and sang.

   b. they brought her through the tunnel and then up through their hole.

   c. she couldn't feel Jessica.

   d. she fell right into the well.

   e. they discovered that Jessica was about 20 feet down in the well.

◆ **REMEMBERING DETAILS**

One word in each sentence is not correct. Find the word and cross it out. Write the correct word.

1. Jessica McClure was 18 ~~years~~ *months* old.

2. A well was in the kitchen of the daycare center.

3. When Jessica fell, she fell right into the water.

4. Jessica's mother ran to a phone and wrote 911.

5. The men said, "We're going to drill a cover next to the well."

6. The men had to drill through soft rock.

7. At 8 P.M. on Friday, men reached Jessica and brought her down from the well.

8. Then doctors rushed her to the hospital.

9. A doctor at the hospital said, "Jessica is lucky she's very old."

10. Jessica doesn't remember the 58 days she was in the well.

4. DISCUSSION

The doctor said, "Jessica is lucky she's very young. She's not going to remember this very well."

Think back to the time when you were very young. Is there an experience you remember? Draw a picture of it on your own paper. Then show your drawing to a small group of classmates. Tell the people in your group about your experience.

Here is what one student drew. What do you think this student's experience was?

5. WRITING

Read this story. It is in the present tense. On your own paper, write the story again in the past tense.

Jessica is playing at a daycare center. Suddenly she falls into a well. She falls about 20 feet and can't get out of the well. Men from the fire department come. They can't go down into the well because it is too narrow.

The men decide to drill a hole next to the well. For the next 58 hours, the men drill the hole. Their job is very difficult because they are drilling through solid rock. Finally, they reach Jessica and bring her up from the well. Jessica's foot and forehead are badly injured, but she is alive. Everyone is very happy.

Jessica was playing at a daycare center. . . .

UNIT
9

1. PRE-READING

Look at the picture.

▸ How old is the man?

▸ How does he feel?

▸ How much money is he holding in his hand?

Read the title of the story. Look at the picture again.

▸ What do you think this story is about?

▸ Can you guess what happens?

Pay It Forward

In 1971, when Larry Stewart was 22 years old, he lost his job. For weeks he drove from city to city and looked for work. He found nothing. In a small town in Mississippi, his car ran out of gas and he ran out of money. He couldn't pay for a hotel room, so he slept in his car. He had no money to buy food, so he got really hungry. For two days, he ate nothing at all.

Early in the morning, Larry went to a small restaurant. Only one man was working there; he was the restaurant's owner. Larry ate a big breakfast. When the owner gave him the bill, Larry reached into his back pocket. "Oh, no!" he said. "I lost my wallet!" Of course, that wasn't true; Larry's wallet was in his car, but there was no money in it.

The owner bent down and reached under Larry's table. When he stood up, he had a 20-dollar bill in his hand. "I think you dropped this," he said. He put the money in Larry's hand. "Yes, I think I did," Larry said. He paid for his breakfast, then pushed his car to a gas station and filled the tank.

Larry decided to drive to Kansas City, Missouri, because he had a cousin there. "Maybe my cousin can help me find work," Larry thought. On the way to Kansas City, Larry thought about the restaurant owner. "He didn't really find that 20 dollars under my table," Larry decided. "He gave me *his* money."

In Kansas City, Larry found a job. Later he started a cable TV business, and it was a success. Nine years after he arrived in Kansas City, Larry was a rich man.

One day Larry went to a restaurant in Kansas City and ordered a hamburger for lunch. The waitress who took his order looked tired. Larry thought back to 1971, when he was tired, hungry, and out of work. He thought about the small restaurant in Mississippi and the man who had given him 20 dollars. When the waitress brought the bill, Larry gave her 20 dollars. "Keep the change," he told her. The waitress started to cry. "Thank you, sir," she said. "Thank you very much."

When Larry left the restaurant, he went to his bank and got some 100-dollar bills. All day he walked around Kansas City with the money. When he saw people who looked sad or poor, he gave them a 100-dollar bill. At the end of the day, he felt wonderful.

Larry had a new hobby: giving money away. Sometimes he gave 100-dollar bills to people on the street. Sometimes he went to fast-food restaurants or Laundromats and gave money to people there. He returned to the restaurant in Mississippi and gave the owner an envelope with $10,000 in it. When the man opened the envelope, he tried to hand it back. "No, sir," Larry told him. "I came to pay you back." Altogether, Larry gave away more than one million dollars.

"We are here on earth to help one another," Larry said. "Help the people who helped you. Help others, too. Don't just pay it back. Pay it forward."

2. VOCABULARY

Complete the sentences with the words below.

change	order	~~ran out of~~	success	tank

1. Larry _____ *ran out of* _____ money, so he couldn't pay for food or a hotel room.

2. He pushed his car to a gas station and filled the _____ with gas.

3. Larry's cable TV business made him a rich man. It was a _____.

4. "I'll have a hamburger," Larry told the waitress who took his _____.

5. Larry gave the waitress 20 dollars for his hamburger. She didn't give him any money back because he told her, "Keep the _____."

3. COMPREHENSION

◆ **REVIEWING THE STORY**

Write the missing words. Then read the story again and check your answers.

When Larry Stewart was a young man, he lost his ___*job*___ and
1.
couldn't find work. A restaurant _____ gave him 20 dollars.
2.
Larry used the money to buy breakfast and gas. Then he _____
3.
to Kansas City, Missouri. He started a cable TV _____ there
4.
and became a rich man.

After Larry became rich, he began giving _____ away. He
5.
gave 100-dollar _____ to people on the street. He also gave
6.
money to people in _____ restaurants and Laundromats.
7.
Altogether, he gave away _____ than one million dollars. "Don't
8.
just pay it back," Larry said. "Pay it _____, too."
9.

◆ **UNDERSTANDING CAUSE AND EFFECT**

**Find the best way to complete each sentence. Write the letter of the answer
on the line.**

1. Larry lost his job, so ___*b*___

2. He couldn't pay for a hotel room,
   so _____

3. He had no money to pay for
   breakfast, so _____

4. The restaurant owner wanted to
   help Larry, so _____

5. Larry wanted to help people who
   looked sad or poor, so _____

a. he told the restaurant owner, "Oh,
no! I lost my wallet!"

b. he drove from city to city and
looked for work.

c. he gave them 100-dollar bills.

d. he gave him 20 dollars.

e. he slept in his car.

◆ **FINDING INFORMATION**

**Read each question. Find the answer in the paragraphs on the next page
and circle it. Write the number of the question above the answer.**

1. In what year did Larry lose his job?
2. How old was he?
3. How long did he look for work?
4. Where did his car run out of gas?
5. Why did he sleep in his car?

6. For how many days did he eat nothing?
7. When did he go to a small restaurant?
8. How many men were working there?
9. What did Larry eat?
10. What did he say when the owner gave him the bill?

In (1971), when Larry Stewart was 22 years old, he lost his job. For weeks he drove from city to city and looked for work. He found nothing. In a small town in Mississippi, his car ran out of gas and he ran out of money. He couldn't pay for a hotel room, so he slept in his car. He had no money to buy food, so he got really hungry. For two days, he ate nothing at all.

Early in the morning, Larry went to a small restaurant. Only one man was working there; he was the restaurant's owner. Larry ate a big breakfast. When the owner gave him the bill, Larry reached into his back pocket. "I lost my wallet!" he said.

4. DISCUSSION/WRITING

Larry said, "Help the people who helped you." Who is someone who helped you?

A. Fill in the chart below. Write the name of someone who helped you (in a big way or in a small way). In a sentence or two, explain how he or she helped you. Then share your writing with a partner.

NAME	HOW HE/SHE HELPED ME

B. On your own paper, write a thank-you letter to the person who helped you. Here is what one student wrote.

Dear Maria,

Thank you for telling me about the English class. I go every Monday, Wednesday, and Friday, and my English is improving.

Antonia

1. PRE-READING

Look at the picture.

▸ Where are these people?

▸ What is on the shelves behind the man?

▸ What is the man doing?

Read the title of the story. Look at the picture again.

▸ What do you think this story is about?

Please Pass the Bird Brains

Do you have a headache? Eat some bird brains for dinner, and your headache will go away. Do you want beautiful skin? Put a spoonful of ground pearls into your soup. Your skin will be beautiful. Is your hair turning gray? Eat black rice every day, and you won't have gray hair.

"Eat bird brains, pearls, and black rice?" some people ask. "How strange!" But for many Chinese people, bird brains, pearls, and black rice are not strange things to eat; they are good things to eat. They are good medicines, too.

Many Chinese believe that food can be medicine. They believe that eating bird brains, for example, stops headaches, soup with ground pearls is good for the skin, and black rice stops hair from turning gray.

Food that is medicine is called *medicinal food*. The Chinese have eaten medicinal food and spices for centuries. Ginger, for example, is a common spice in Chinese cooking. Ginger gives food a nice flavor. The Chinese began to use ginger many years ago. They used ginger not because it tasted good; they used ginger because it was medicinal. Ginger, they thought, was good for the digestion. It also helped people who had colds. Pepper and garlic, too, were probably medicines a long time ago.

Some people don't believe that food and spices are good medicines. They want to buy their medicine in drugstores, not in supermarkets. Other people want to try medicinal food. They say, "Maybe medicinal food can't help me. But it can't hurt me, either."

People can try medicinal food at a Chinese restaurant in San Francisco, California. The restaurant serves only medicinal food. The menus at the restaurant have a list of dinners. Next to each dinner, there is information about the food. The information helps people order. "Queen's Secret," for example, is one dinner at the restaurant. Meat from a chicken with black skin is in the dinner. It is for women who want to look young. "Lover's Soup" is for people whose marriages are unhappy. The soup has dinosaur bones in it, and it helps people's love lives. Even the drinks at the restaurant are medicinal. One drink is deer tail wine. It gives people more energy.

Alan Lau is the owner of the restaurant. Mr. Lau says, "Some people try medicinal food one time and then they say, 'It didn't work.' But think about this: When your doctor prescribes medicine, you take the medicine for five days, or for ten days, or maybe for weeks. It's the same with medicinal food. You have to eat the food many times before it begins to help." Mr. Lau believes that medicinal food works; he eats medicinally every day.

Mr. Lau also owns a store that sells medicinal food. The store is next to the restaurant. People who want to cook medicinal food at home can buy it at the store. In the picture, Mr. Lau is working at his store. He is weighing something for a customer. Is it a spice? Is it medicine? Or is it both?

2. VOCABULARY

Complete the sentences with the words below.

centuries	common	digestion	~~ground~~

1. For beautiful skin, some people eat very, very small pieces of pearls. They put

   _____*ground*_____ pearls in their soup.

2. The Chinese probably used pepper as a medicine hundreds of years ago. They have

   eaten medicinal food and spices for _____.

3. The Chinese use ginger often. It is a _____ spice in Chinese cooking.

4. Ginger helps the stomach. It is good for the _____.

3. COMPREHENSION

◆ **UNDERSTANDING THE MAIN IDEA**

Circle the letter of the best answer.

1. "Please Pass the Bird Brains" is about

    a. eating bird brains.

    b. Chinese medicinal food.

    c. delicious food and spices.

2. People who like medicinal food say,

    a. "Food and spices can be good medicine."

    b. "I buy medicine only in drugstores."

    c. "Eating bird brains is strange."

◆ **REMEMBERING DETAILS**

Read the list of medicinal foods on the left. Why do people who eat medicinally eat them? Look in the story for the answers. Match each food with the reason people eat it. Write the letter of the answer on the line.

_c_ **1.** bird brains	**a.** for digestion and colds
_____ **2.** soup with ground pearls	**b.** for more energy
_____ **3.** black rice	**c.** to stop headaches
_____ **4.** ginger	**d.** to stop hair from turning gray
_____ **5.** chicken with black skin	**e.** for a good love life
_____ **6.** dinosaur bones	**f.** for beautiful skin
_____ **7.** deer tails	**g.** to look young

◆ **FINDING MORE INFORMATION**

Read each sentence on the left. Which sentence on the right gives you more information? Write the letter of the answer on the line.

_d_ **1.** Food that is medicine is called medicinal food.	**a.** Next to each dinner, there is information about the food.
_____ **2.** The menus at the restaurant have a list of dinners.	**b.** He eats medicinally every day.
_____ **3.** Mr. Lau believes that medicinal food works.	**c.** It is next to the restaurant.
_____ **4.** Mr. Lau also owns a store that sells medicinal food.	**d.** The Chinese have eaten it for centuries.

4. DISCUSSION

Not only the Chinese use medicinal food. People all over the world use medicinal food and home remedies. For example, when someone has an earache, people in Italy put a little warm olive oil in the ear. Putting olive oil in the ear is a home remedy for an earache. Do your classmates use medicinal food and home remedies?

A. Ask a classmate, "Do you know any home remedies for these problems?"

- an earache
- a headache
- hiccups
- a cold
- a stomachache
- a backache
- a sore throat
- a burn
- an insect bite

B. Share information about medicinal food and home remedies with the class.

5. WRITING

Imagine this: There is a special medicinal food. It is not for headaches or stomachaches. This medicinal food is for problems. When you eat it, your problems go away. You went to the store, bought the medicinal food, and ate it.

Which problems went away? Write about them. Here is what one student wrote.

I had three problems. My English was not good. I didn't have enough money. I didn't have a boyfriend. Then I ate the medicinal food. Now my English is perfect. I got a new job, and I make $50,000 a year. I have plenty of money. I also have a boyfriend. He is very handsome. That medicinal food was great!

1. PRE-READING

Look at the picture.

▸ What is unusual about the way the women are playing the piano?

▸ Why do you think they are playing the piano together?

Read the title of the story. Look at the picture again.

▸ Do you think the women are old friends or new friends?

▸ What do you think this story is about?

▸ Can you guess what happens?

Margaret Patrick . . . Meet Ruth Eisenberg

Ruth Eisenberg and Margaret Patrick played the piano together for several years. They gave concerts in the United States and in Canada, and they were often on TV. They were famous.

Why were they famous? They played the piano well, but they were not famous because they played well. They were famous because Mrs. Eisenberg played the piano with only her right hand, and Mrs. Patrick played the piano with only her left hand. They sat next to each other and played the piano together. Mrs. Eisenberg played one part of the music, and Mrs. Patrick played the other part.

Mrs. Eisenberg and Mrs. Patrick didn't always play the piano with only one hand. When they were younger, they played with two hands. Mrs. Patrick was a piano teacher. She taught hundreds of students. She taught her own children, too. Then, when she was 69 years old, Mrs. Patrick had a stroke. She couldn't move or speak. Gradually she got better, but her right side was still very weak. She couldn't play the piano anymore. She was very sad.

Playing the piano was Mrs. Eisenberg's hobby. She often played five or six hours a day. Then, when she was 80 years old, she, too, had a stroke. She couldn't move the left side of her body, so she couldn't play the piano anymore. She was very sad.

A few months after her stroke, Mrs. Eisenberg went to a senior citizens' center. There were a lot of activities at the center, and Mrs. Eisenberg wanted to keep busy. Mrs. Patrick wanted to keep busy, too. A few weeks later, she went to the same center. The director was showing her around the center when Mrs. Patrick saw a piano. She looked sadly at the piano. "Is anything wrong?" the director asked. "No," Mrs. Patrick answered. "The piano brings back memories. Before my stroke, I played the piano." The director looked at Mrs. Patrick's weak right hand and said, "Wait here. I'll be right back." A few minutes later, the director came back with Mrs. Eisenberg. "Margaret Patrick," the director said. "Meet Ruth Eisenberg. Before her stroke, she played the piano, too. She has a good right hand, and you have a good left hand. I think you two can do something wonderful together."

"Do you know Chopin's Waltz in D flat?" Mrs. Eisenberg asked Mrs. Patrick. "Yes," Mrs. Patrick answered. The two women sat down at the piano and began to play. Mrs. Eisenberg used only her right hand, and Mrs. Patrick used only her left hand. The music sounded good. The women discovered that they loved the same music. Together they began to play the music they loved. They were not sad anymore.

Mrs. Patrick said, "Sometimes God closes a door and then opens a window. I lost my music, but I found Ruth. Now I have my music again. I have my friend Ruth, too."

Which words have the same meaning as the words in *italics*? Write the letter of the answer on the line.

___b___ **1.** Mrs. Patrick got better. It happened *slowly*.

_____ **2.** Her right side was *not strong*.

_____ **3.** Mrs. Eisenberg enjoyed playing the piano. It was *something she did in her free time*.

_____ **4.** Mrs. Patrick and Mrs. Eisenberg were both *more than 65 years old*.

_____ **5.** There were a lot of *things to do* at the senior center.

a. senior citizens

b. gradually

c. activities

d. weak

e. her hobby

43

3. COMPREHENSION

◆ **UNDERSTANDING CONNECTIONS**

Find the best way to complete each sentence. Write the letter of the answer on the line.

1. Mrs. Eisenberg played the piano with her right hand, and ___*b*___

2. Mrs. Eisenberg played one part of the music, and _____

3. Mrs. Patrick was a piano teacher, and _____

4. Mrs. Patrick was 69 years old when she had a stroke, and _____

5. Mrs. Patrick said that sometimes God closes a door, and _____

6. Mrs. Patrick had her music back, and _____

a. Mrs. Eisenberg played the piano as a hobby.

b. Mrs. Patrick played with her left hand.

c. then God opens a window.

d. Mrs. Patrick played the other part.

e. she had a new friend, too.

f. Mrs. Eisenberg was 80.

◆ **MAKING INFERENCES**

Find the best way to complete each sentence. Write the letter of the answer on the line. (The answers are not in the story; you have to guess.)

1. Mrs. Eisenberg and Mrs. Patrick gave concerts in the United States and in Canada, so probably ___*b*___

2. Mrs. Patrick taught the piano to hundreds of students, so probably _____

3. Mrs. Patrick and Mrs. Eisenberg went to the same senior citizens' center, so probably _____

4. Both women knew Chopin's Waltz in D flat, so probably _____

a. they lived in the same city.

b. they traveled often.

c. they liked classical music.

d. she was a piano teacher for many years.

Imagine this: You want to tell the story "Margaret Patrick . . . Meet Ruth Eisenberg" to a friend. You want to tell the story quickly, in only six sentences. Which six sentences tell the story best? Check (✓) the answer.

☐ **1.** Two women played the piano. One woman was a piano teacher; she taught hundreds of students and her own children, too. The other woman played the piano as a hobby; she often played five or six hours a day. Both women had a stroke and couldn't play the piano anymore. They were very sad. The women wanted to keep busy, so they went to a senior citizens' center.

☐ **2.** Two women had a stroke and couldn't play the piano anymore. One woman couldn't use her left arm, and the other woman couldn't use her right arm. One day the women met at a senior citizens' center. They discovered they could play the piano together. They began to give concerts. One woman played one part of the music with her left hand, and the other woman played the other part with her right hand.

4. DISCUSSION/WRITING

Mrs. Patrick and Mrs. Eisenberg had a lot in common: They both played the piano, they loved the same music, and they both had a stroke. What about you and your partner? Do you have anything in common?

Talk with a partner to find out what you have in common. You will need to ask each other questions—for example, "Are you a good dancer?" or "When is your birthday?" On the lines below, make a list of three things you and your partner have in common. Then share your list with the class. (Do not write about things you can see—for example, *We both have brown eyes*.) Here is what one student wrote.

We both have two brothers but no sisters.
We both like to play soccer.
We were both born in 1987.

_____

_____

_____

UNIT
12

1. PRE-READING

Look at the picture.

▸ Where is this?

▸ What do you think the people are doing?

Read the title of the story. Look at the picture again.

▸ What does the expression *finders keepers* mean?

▸ What do you think this story is about?

▸ Can you guess what happens?

Finders Keepers?

Mel Kiser was driving along a busy highway in Columbus, Ohio. He saw an armored truck a few cars ahead of him. Suddenly the back doors of the armored truck opened, and a blue plastic bag fell out of the truck. A car in front of Mr. Kiser hit the bag. The bag ripped, and money spilled out. Then another bag fell out of the truck, and another. Money was flying everywhere.

At first, drivers thought the green papers on the highway were leaves. Then they realized that the green papers were not leaves—they were money! Drivers slammed on their brakes and stopped right in the middle of the highway. People jumped out of their cars and began picking up money. They were putting 10-, 20-, and 100-dollar bills into their pockets. One man was yelling, "Money, money, money! It's all free! Grab some while you can!"

Mr. Kiser also got out of his car. He grabbed a plastic bag of money, put the bag in his car, and drove away.

Later Mr. Kiser counted the money. He had $57,000. For the next two hours, Mr. Kiser thought about the money. He dreamed about spending it. He needed a new furnace for his house. He wanted to take a vacation in Florida. But he decided to return the money. He drove to the police station and gave the police the $57,000.

Mr. Kiser returned $57,000, and other people returned money, too. But over one million dollars were still missing. The armored truck company offered a 10 percent reward. "If you return $1,000, for example, we will pay you $100," the company said. Mel Kiser had returned $57,000, so the company gave him a reward of $5,700. A few more people returned money and got rewards, but most of the money—almost a million dollars—was still missing.

Then the armored truck company got some help. A man telephoned and said, "I was driving along the highway when I saw a traffic jam ahead," the man said. "I didn't want to be in the traffic jam, so I took the next exit and got off the highway. Then I saw the money. People were running everywhere. I had a camera in my car, and I took some pictures. Would you like the pictures?"

"Yes!" answered the armored truck company. The company gave the pictures to the police. The police looked closely at the pictures. They looked at the cars, the license plates, and the people's faces. They tried to find the people who had taken the money, but they didn't have much luck.

One man who had taken money telephoned a Columbus newspaper. The man did not give his name. "I took two bags of money," he said. "I'm going to take the money and leave Columbus. I have enough money for the rest of my life."

2. VOCABULARY

Complete the sentences with the words below.

~~armored truck~~	grabbing	ripped	slammed on their brakes

1. The truck ahead of Mel Kiser was small and strong, and it carried money. It was an _armored truck_ .

2. When cars hit the plastic bags, the bags broke and opened. The bags _____.

3. When the drivers saw money flying everywhere, they stopped suddenly. They

    _____.

4. People were running everywhere and taking money. They were _____

    10-, 20-, and 100-dollar bills.

3. COMPREHENSION

◆ **REMEMBERING DETAILS**

One word in each sentence is not correct. Find the word and cross it out. Write the correct word.

1. Mel Kiser was driving along a ~~quiet~~ _busy_ highway in Columbus, Ohio.

2. He saw an armored bus a few cars ahead of him.

3. Suddenly the back doors of the armored truck closed.

4. A blue paper bag fell out of the truck.

5. The bag ripped, and leaves spilled out.

6. People jumped out of their houses and began picking up money.

7. They were putting 10-, 30-, and 100-dollar bills into their pockets.

8. The armored truck company offered a 10 percent tax.

9. More people returned money, but almost a million pennies were still missing.

◆ **UNDERSTANDING TIME RELATIONSHIPS**

Find the best way to complete each sentence. Write the letter of the answer on the line.

1. When the back doors of the armored truck opened, __c__

2. When cars hit the plastic bags, _____

3. When drivers realized that the green papers were money, _____

4. When Mr. Kiser went to the police station, _____

5. When the armored truck company offered a reward, _____

a. they slammed on their brakes.

b. the bags ripped.

c. blue plastic bags fell out of the truck.

d. more people returned money.

e. he returned $57,000.

◆ **MAKING INFERENCES**

Find the best way to complete each sentence. Write the letter of the answer on the line. (The answers are not in the story; you have to guess.)

1. There is a busy highway in Columbus, Ohio, so probably ___b___

2. The driver of the armored truck didn't stop, so probably _____

3. Mel Kiser needed a furnace, so probably _____

4. Mel Kiser returned all the money, so probably _____

5. One man said, "I have enough money for the rest of my life," so probably _____

a. he didn't realize that money was falling from the truck.

b. Columbus is a big city.

c. he found a lot of money.

d. he is an honest man.

e. the weather is sometimes cold in Ohio.

4. DISCUSSION

Imagine this: You are walking in a big city in your native country. You find a bag on the sidewalk. There is $57,000 in the bag.

What will you do with the money? Check (✓) one answer.

☐ I will keep the money.

☐ I will give the money to the police. I will tell the police, "Try to find the owner of the money."

☐ I will try to find the owner of the money myself.

☐ I will give the money to poor people.

☐ _____

(Write your own answer.)

Explain your answer in a small group.

5. WRITING

Imagine that you see bags of money on a highway. What will you do? Complete the story on your own paper.

Last week I was driving along a busy highway when I saw an armored truck a few cars ahead of me. Suddenly the back doors of the truck opened, and a blue plastic bag fell out of the truck. A car in front of me hit the bag. The bag ripped, and money spilled out. Then another bag fell out of the truck, and another. Money was flying everywhere. I . . .

UNIT 13

1. PRE-READING

Look at the picture.

▸ The things in the photo are for sale at a flea market. What kinds of things can people buy at flea markets?

▸ Are there flea markets in your native country? If so, do you sometimes shop there? What kinds of things do you buy?

Read the title of the story. Look at the picture again.

▸ What do you think this story is about?

▸ Can you guess what happens?

The Husband

Sharon Clark will never forget the day she met Giovanni Vigliotto. She was working in Indiana, as the manager of a large flea market. Early one morning, he walked into her office. "I'd like to rent some space at the flea market," he said. "I have a lot of used things to sell. Do you have any space?"

"Yes, I do," she answered.

When the flea market closed at the end of the day, Giovanni invited Sharon to have dinner with him. She was 43 years old, divorced, and a little lonely. She said yes.

For the next four months, Sharon saw Giovanni often. He was not a handsome man—he was short and heavy, and he had a big nose. But he was intelligent, polite, and kind. She fell in love with him. "Marry me," Giovanni said.

Sharon thought it over. Her mind told her, "Don't do it. You don't know him well enough." But her heart told her, "Do it. Take a chance." Sharon listened to her heart and married Giovanni.

After they got married, Giovanni said he wanted to move to Canada. "I have a beautiful house there," he said. "Let's sell your house and move to Canada." Sharon sold her house and made a profit of $55,000. She wanted to take her furniture to Canada, so she and Giovanni rented a truck. "I'll drive the truck, and you can drive your car," he said. "You'd better give me the $55,000. It's dangerous for a woman to travel with that much money."

"You're right," Sharon agreed, and she gave Giovanni the $55,000.

On the way from Indiana to Canada, Giovanni told Sharon he had to stop in Ohio on business. "You go on ahead," he told her. They decided to meet at a hotel in Canada.

Giovanni never arrived at the hotel. At first Sharon was worried. "Maybe Giovanni was in an accident," she thought. She called the police in Ohio. "No," the police said, "Giovanni Vigliotto wasn't in an accident here." So where was Giovanni? He was gone, and so were her furniture and her money.

Sharon was angry. She wanted her money and her furniture back. She wanted to find Giovanni. "I met him at a flea market," she thought. "Maybe he's at a flea market somewhere."

For months Sharon went to flea markets all over the United States. At a flea market in Florida, she found Giovanni. He was selling used furniture. Some of it was hers. Sharon called the police.

When the police arrested Giovanni, Sharon's story was in newspapers and on TV. A woman in New Jersey called the police. "Giovanni is my husband, too!" she said. Then another woman called the police, and another, and another. "Giovanni is my husband!" the women said. All the women told similar stories: They met Giovanni at a flea market; they sold their houses; he took their furniture and their money. Altogether, 105 women were married to Giovanni.

A judge sentenced Giovanni to 34 years in prison. "I want you to stay in prison for a long time," the judge told Giovanni. "I want to be sure there will be no wife number 106."

2. VOCABULARY

Which words have the same meaning as the words in italics? Write the letter of the answer on the line.

___e___ **1.** Giovanni said, "*I want* to rent some space."

_____ **2.** "*You should* give me the $55,000," Giovanni told Sharon.

_____ **3.** Sharon said, "*You're right*."

_____ **4.** Sharon looked for Giovanni *in many places* in the United States.

_____ **5.** The police *took* Giovanni *away*.

_____ **6.** All the women's stories were *almost the same*.

a. arrested

b. You'd better

c. similar

d. all over

e. I'd like

f. I agree

3. COMPREHENSION

◆ **REMEMBERING DETAILS**

Read the summary of the story "The Husband." There are 11 mistakes in the summary. Find the mistakes and cross them out. Write the correct words. (The first one is done for you.)

Sharon Clark was the ~~owner~~ *manager* of a large fruit market. Giovanni rented space at the market because he had some new things to sell. At the end of the day, he invited Sharon to have dessert with him.

For the next four weeks, Sharon saw Giovanni often, and she fell in love with him. She didn't know him well, but she listened to her mind and married him.

Giovanni said he wanted to move to Mexico because he had a house there. So Sharon sold her house and made a profit of $5,000. She and Giovanni rented a car, and he drove away with her furniture and her money. He never arrived in Canada.

Sharon found Giovanni at a flea market in California and called the police. After the police arrested Giovanni, many women told similar stories about him. Altogether, he had 55 wives.

◆ **FINDING MORE INFORMATION**

Read each sentence on the left. Which sentence on the right gives you more information? Write the letter of the answer on the line.

__c__ **1.** Giovanni was not a handsome man.	**a.** He said he had a beautiful house there.
_____ **2.** Giovanni wanted to move to Canada.	**b.** They met Giovanni at a flea market; they sold their houses; he took their furniture and their money.
_____ **3.** Giovanni was selling used furniture.	
_____ **4.** All of the women told similar stories.	**c.** He was short and heavy, and he had a big nose.
	d. Some of it was Sharon's.

◆ **UNDERSTANDING TIME AND PLACE**

Read the phrases from the story. Which phrases tell you *when* something happened? Write them in the *WHEN* column. Which phrases tell you *where* something happened? Write them in the *WHERE* column.

▸ early one morning
▸ at the flea market
▸ at the end of the day
▸ for the next four months

▸ after they got married
▸ on the way from Indiana to Canada
▸ at the hotel
▸ all over the United States

WHEN	WHERE
early one morning	_____
_____	_____
_____	_____

4. DISCUSSION

Sharon knew Giovanni for four months. Then she married him. But her mind told her, "Don't do it. You don't know him well enough."

How long (how many weeks, months, or years) should you know someone before you get married? Write your answer on the line. Then explain your answer in a small group. If you are married, tell the class how long you knew your husband or wife before you got married.

_____

5. WRITING

Sharon met Giovanni at a flea market. When the flea market closed at the end of the day, Giovanni invited Sharon to have dinner with him.

Interview a classmate, friend, or relative who is married. Ask, "How did you meet your husband (or wife)?" Write the story on your own paper. Here is what one student wrote.

Every Sunday morning, my mother and her family went for a walk near the seaside. What they didn't know was that a young sailor was looking at them from a ship with his binoculars. My father fell in love with my mother. One Sunday he introduced himself to her. That happened 52 years ago, and they have been happily married for 50 years.

UNIT 14

1. PRE-READING

Look at the picture.

▶ Why do you think the girl has no hair?

▶ How do you think she feels?

▶ What is she holding?

Read the title of the story. Then look at the picture again.

▶ What is an auction?

▶ Can you guess what happens?

The Auction

Katie Fisher was excited. It was July 15—the day of the animal auction. "Today I'm going to sell my lamb," she thought.

Seventeen-year-old Katie lived on a farm in Madison County, Ohio. Every July there was an animal auction in Madison County. Children from farms all over the county brought their best animals to an arena. They sold their animals to the farmer who paid the highest price. "I hope I get a good price for my lamb," Katie thought.

On the afternoon of the auction, Katie walked into the center of the arena with her lamb. People were a little surprised when they saw Katie. She had no hair. She had no hair because of chemotherapy. Katie had cancer. The chemotherapy had stopped the cancer, and Katie felt much better. But Katie's parents had a lot of medical bills to pay. Katie wanted to sell her lamb and pay some of her medical bills.

The auctioneer decided to say a few words about Katie. "This young lady needs money for her medical bills," the auctioneer said. "Let's give her a good price for her lamb." Then the auctioneer began the auction.

"Who'll give me one dollar a pound for this lamb?" he began.

"One dollar!" a farmer said.

"I hear one dollar," the auctioneer said. "Who'll give me two dollars a pound?"

"Two dollars!" another farmer said.

"I hear two dollars," the auctioneer continued. "Who'll give me three dollars?"

The auctioneer continued to raise the price of the lamb, and the farmers continued to offer more money. Finally, Katie's lamb sold for twelve dollars a pound.

Katie was happy. Lambs usually sold for two dollars a pound, but her lamb sold for twelve dollars a pound! She took her lamb to the farmer who bought it. The farmer paid Katie for the lamb and then said something surprising: "Keep the lamb," he told Katie. "Sell it again."

Katie walked back into the center of the arena with her lamb. Smiling, the auctioneer said, "Well, I guess I have to sell this lamb again." A second farmer bought the lamb, this time for eight dollars a pound.

When the auctioneer sold the lamb for the second time, something amazing happened. The farm families in the arena began chanting, "Sell it again! Sell it again!" When Katie took her lamb to the second farmer, he paid her for the lamb. Then he smiled and said, "You heard the people. Keep the lamb. Sell it again."

Katie walked back into the center of the arena with her lamb, and the crowd cheered. The auctioneer sold Katie's lamb again . . . and again . . . and again. Every time the auctioneer sold the lamb, the crowd chanted, "Sell it again! Sell it again!"

That afternoon the farmers of Madison County, Ohio, bought Katie's lamb 36 times. All 36 farmers paid Katie, but not one farmer took the lamb. Katie went home with $16,000—enough money to pay all her medical bills. She also went home with her lamb.

2. VOCABULARY

Complete the sentences with the words below.

auctioneer	chanted	cheered	~~crowd~~

1. Hundreds of farm families went to the animal auction. There was a big
   _____crowd_____ of people.

2. Before he began the auction, the _____ said a few words about Katie.

3. The farm families repeated the same words. "Sell it again! Sell it again!" they

   _____ .

4. The people at the auction were happy when Katie walked back into the center of the

   arena with her lamb, so they _____ .

3. COMPREHENSION

◆ **REMEMBERING DETAILS**

One word in each sentence is not correct. Find the word and cross it out. Write the correct word.

1. Katie Fisher was excited because she was going to sell her ~~cow~~. *lamb*

2. Seven-year-old Katie lived on a farm in Madison County, Ohio.

3. Every December there was an animal auction in Madison County.

4. Children from farms all over the world brought their best animals to an arena.

5. They sold their animals to the farmer who paid the lowest price.

6. Lambs usually sold for two cents a pound, but Katie's lamb sold for twelve dollars a pound.

7. Katie took her lamb to the auctioneer who bought it.

8. The farmer thanked Katie for the lamb and then said, "Keep the lamb."

◆ **UNDERSTANDING CAUSE AND EFFECT**

Find the best way to complete each sentence. Write the letter of the answer on the line.

1. Katie wanted to sell her lamb ___e___

2. The people in the arena were surprised when they saw Katie _____

3. The second farmer who bought the lamb told Katie, "You heard the people" _____

4. Katie got $16,000 for her lamb _____

5. Katie went home with her lamb _____

a. because the farm families were chanting, "Sell it again."

b. because the farmers bought it 36 times.

c. because the farmers who bought the lamb didn't take it.

d. because she had no hair.

e. because she needed money for medical bills.

◆ **UNDERSTANDING A SUMMARY**

Imagine this: You want to tell the story "The Auction" to a friend. You want to tell the story quickly, in only four sentences. Which four sentences tell the story best? Check (✓) your answer.

☐ 1. A seventeen-year-old girl who had cancer needed money for her medical bills. She decided to sell her lamb at an auction in Madison County, Ohio. The auction happens every July in Madison County. Farm children take their best animals to an arena and sell them to the farmer who pays the highest price.

☐ 2. A seventeen-year-old girl who had cancer needed money for her medical bills. She decided to sell her lamb at an auction. Every time she sold her lamb, the farmer who bought it didn't take it. She sold the lamb 36 times and went home with $16,000—enough money to pay all her medical bills.

4. DISCUSSION

The farm families did something kind for Katie. People do kind things every day. For example: They give money to poor people; they help people who are lost; they open doors for people who are carrying packages.

Did someone do something kind for you? Did *you* do something kind for someone? In a small group, tell your classmates about it.

5. WRITING

Katie Fisher keeps a diary. Every night, she writes down what happened that day. What did Katie write on the night of July 15?

On your own paper, finish the page in Katie's diary.

> July 15
>   This afternoon I went to the arena to sell my lamb. I walked into the center of the arena. The auctioneer told the people I needed money for medical bills. Then he began the auction. The lamb sold for twelve dollars a pound! I took my lamb to the farmer who bought it. He...

UNIT 15

1. PRE-READING

Look at the picture.

▶ How do you think this woman feels?

▶ What is the woman doing with the money?

▶ Why do you think she is doing that?

Read the title of the story. Look at the picture again.

▶ What do you think this story is about?

▶ Can you guess what happens?

Money to Burn

Lillian Beard whistled and smiled while she worked. "Why are you so happy?" her co-workers asked her.

"Last week I got my income tax refund," Lillian answered. "This morning I went to the bank and cashed the check. I have $462 in my pocket. I'm thinking about the money. How will I spend it?"

After work Lillian came home and decided to wash some clothes. She looked at the jeans she was wearing. They were dirty, so she put them in the washing machine, too. Ten minutes later, she remembered: "The money! It's still in the pocket of my jeans!" Lillian ran to the washing machine and took out the jeans. The money was still in the pocket, but it was wet. Lillian put the money on the kitchen table to dry.

A few hours later, the money was still wet. "Hmm," Lillian thought. "How can I dry this money?" Then Lillian had an idea. She could dry the money in her microwave oven! Lillian put the money in the microwave, set the timer for five minutes, and left the kitchen.

When Lillian came back a few minutes later, she saw a fire in the microwave. She opened the oven door, blew out the fire, and looked at her money. The money was burned.

The next day, Lillian took the burned money to the bank. A teller at the bank told her, "If I can see the numbers on the burned bills, I can give you new money." Unfortunately, the teller found numbers on only a few bills. The teller took those bills and gave Lillian $17.

A newspaper reporter heard about the burned money. He wrote a story about Lillian for the newspaper. Several people read the story and called the newspaper. "Tell Ms. Beard to send the burned money to the U.S. Department of Treasury," the people said. "Maybe she can get her money back."

Every year about 30,000 people send damaged money to the Treasury Department. Experts there look carefully at the damaged money. Sometimes they can give people new money for the damaged money. Once a farmer dropped his wallet in a field, and a cow ate his money—thousands of dollars. The farmer killed the cow and sent the cow's stomach, with the money inside, to the Treasury Department. The experts gave the farmer new money.

Lillian sent her money to the Treasury Department. The experts looked at Lillian's burned money and sent her a check for $231.

What did Lillian buy with the money? She didn't buy anything. She gave the $231 to friends who needed money. Lillian said, "When I burned the $462, I thought, 'Well, my money is gone.' The check for $231 was a big surprise. I decided to give the money to my friends. Money is important, but people are more important to me."

2. VOCABULARY

Complete the sentences with the words below.

experts	income	refund	set the timer	teller

1. Lillian works and earns money. She pays tax on the money she earns. She pays

   _____income_____ tax.

2. When Lillian paid her income tax, she gave the government too much money. The government gave her some money back. Lillian got a _____ on her income tax.

3. Lillian wanted the microwave oven to heat the money for five minutes, so she

   _____ for five minutes.

4. People at the Treasury Department know a lot about money. They are _____.

5. Lillian took her burned money to the bank and showed it to someone who worked

   there. The _____ took some of the bills and gave Lillian $17.

3. COMPREHENSION

◆ **REMEMBERING DETAILS**

What did Lillian Beard do with her money? Check (✓) seven answers. (The first one is done for you.)

- ☑ She put it in her pocket.
- ☐ She washed it with her jeans.
- ☐ She put it on the kitchen table to dry.
- ☐ She counted it many times.
- ☐ She burned it in her microwave oven.
- ☐ She showed it to a teller at the bank.
- ☐ She sent it to the Treasury Department.
- ☐ She spent it.
- ☐ She gave it to friends.

◆ **UNDERSTANDING PRONOUNS**

Look at the pronouns. (They are in *italics*.) What do they mean? Write the letter of the answer on the line.

_b_ **1.** Lillian cashed *it*.

_____ **2.** Lillian decided to wash *them*.

_____ **3.** *It* was damaged.

_____ **4.** Lillian set *it* for five minutes.

_____ **5.** *He* wrote a story about Lillian.

_____ **6.** *It* ate a farmer's money.

_____ **7.** *They* looked carefully at Lillian's burned money.

_____ **8.** Lillian gave *them* money.

a. experts at the Treasury Department

b. her income tax refund check

c. her jeans

d. the timer

e. a newspaper reporter

f. a cow

g. her friends

h. Lillian's money

◆ **UNDERSTANDING A SUMMARY**

Imagine this: You want to tell the story "Money to Burn" to a friend. You want to tell the story quickly, in only four sentences. Which four sentences tell the story best? Check (✓) your answer.

- ☐ **1.** A woman who got a $462 income tax refund went to the bank and cashed the check. At work she was very happy because she had $462 in her pocket. After work she went home and washed her jeans. She forgot to take the money out of the pocket, so the money got wet.

2. When a woman washed her jeans, she forgot that she had $462 in the pocket. She tried to dry the wet money in her microwave oven but burned it. She sent the burned money to experts at the U.S. Treasury Department, who mailed the woman a check for $231. The woman gave the money to her friends.

4. DISCUSSION

Lillian Beard lived in the United States, in the state of Indiana. In Indiana, people pay tax on income, houses and land, food they eat in restaurants, things they buy in stores, and tickets for movies and sporting events. What is taxed in your native country? What is taxed in your partner's native country?

First, on the lines below, make a list of things that are taxed in your native country. Then ask a partner what is taxed in his or her native country. Write your partner's list on the lines. Finally, tell the class what you learned about taxes in your partner's native country.

MY COUNTRY   **MY PARTNER'S COUNTRY**

_____   _____

_____   _____

5. WRITING

Look at a coin or bill. Then describe the money in a paragraph on your own paper. Here is what one student wrote.

I have a five-dinar bill from Bahrain. It is worth about 13 American dollars. Its colors are blue and green. On one side of the bill, the language is Arabic. On the other side of the bill, the language is English. If you hold the bill up to the light, you can see a drawing of an ox's head.

USA 41
TOWARD EQUALITY IN OUR SCHOOLS
MENDEZ v. WESTMINSTER 1947

1. PRE-READING

Look at the picture.

▸ What country is the stamp from?

▸ How much does the stamp cost?

▸ What names do you see on the stamp?

▸ What are the two young people doing?

Read the title of the story. Look at the picture again.

▸ What do you think this story is about?

▸ Can you guess what happens?

The School and the Stamp

In October 2007, post offices in the United States began selling a new stamp. On the stamp, there is a drawing of two strong young people with black hair. They are reading a book, and a bright sun is shining on them.

There is a true story behind that stamp. The story begins in 1945 with a man named Gonzalo Mendez.

Gonzalo Mendez was born in Mexico and came to the United States when he was a little boy. He dropped out of school at age ten to become a farm worker. He and his wife, Felicitas, had three children and owned a small but successful café in Santa Ana, California.

In 1945, Gonzalo heard about an asparagus farm that was for rent. The farm was in Westminster, California, about seven miles from Santa Ana. Gonzalo was excited about renting the farm; this was his chance to be a real farmer, not a farm worker. He and Felicitas talked it over, and they decided to move to Westminster.

After the Mendez family moved to Westminster, Felicitas took the three children to an elementary school there. That is when the story behind the stamp really begins. Felicitas found out that her children could not attend the school. They had to attend the "Mexican school."

The "Mexican school" was in an old building. The textbooks were old, too. When the children came home and described the school to their father, he told them, "You will not go to the 'Mexican school.' You will go to the other school."

Gonzalo talked to other Latino parents in Westminster. "The other elementary school is better than the 'Mexican school,'" he told them. "Let's go to court. Let's fight to get our children into that other school."

The Latino parents agreed with Gonzalo: The other elementary school was better in every way. But the "Mexican school" was closer. "Our children will stay at the 'Mexican school,' close to home," the Latino parents told Gonzalo.

So Gonzalo decided to fight alone. He spent all his savings to hire a lawyer, and he went to court.

Latino families in other cities in Southern California heard about Gonzalo Mendez. Their children, too, had to attend "Mexican schools." Four Latino families decided to help Gonzalo. They gave him money for the lawyer and went to court with him.

The judge decided that the Latino families were right: Separate schools for Latino children were unfair. At that time, there were 5,000 Latino children who had to attend "Mexican schools" in Southern California. After the judge's decision, they could attend any school.

The Mendez children went to elementary school and then to high school; some went to college, too.

In 2007, the Mendez family celebrated the new stamp, which they liked very much. They especially liked the way the two young readers bend like plants toward the sun. "That's how it is," they said. "Education brings light into people's lives. This small stamp tells our whole story."

2. VOCABULARY

Which words have the same meaning as the words in italics? Write the letter of the answer on the line.

_d_ **1.** There is a *picture* of two strong young people on the stamp.

_____ **2.** Gonzalo *stopped going to* school when he was ten years old.

_____ **3.** The Mendez children *were students at* the "Mexican school."

_____ **4.** The Latino families in Westminster *thought Gonzalo was right*.

a. dropped out of

b. agreed with Gonzalo

c. attended

d. drawing

3. COMPREHENSION

◆ **UNDERSTANDING THE MAIN IDEAS**

Complete the sentences. Write your answers on the lines.

1. When does the story behind the stamp begin?

   It begins in _____1945_____ with a man named Gonzalo _____.

2. Why was Gonzalo excited about renting the asparagus farm?

   It was his chance to be a real _____, not a

   _____ _____.

3. What did Felicitas do after the Mendez family moved to Westminster?

   She took her _____ to an _____ school there.

4. Where was the "Mexican school"?

   It was in an _____ building.

5. What did Gonzalo Mendez tell the Latino parents in Westminster?

   He said, "Let's _____ to get our children into that other _____."

6. Why did the Latino families in Westminster want their children to stay at

   the "Mexican school"?

   It was _____ to home.

7. How did the four Latino families help Gonzalo?

   They gave him money for the _____ and went to _____ with him.

8. What did the judge decide?

   The judge decided that _____ schools for Latino children

   were _____.

◆ **UNDERSTANDING PRONOUNS**

**Look at the pronouns. (They are in *italics*.) What do they mean? Write the
letter of the answer on the line.**

___a___ 1. *They* began selling a new
stamp in October 2007.

_____ 2. A bright sun is shining on *them*.

_____ 3. *They* had to go to "Mexican
schools."

_____ 4. *They* were old.

_____ 5. Gonzalo talked to *them*.

a. post offices in the United States

b. the textbooks at the "Mexican
school"

c. Latino children in Southern
California

d. the young people on the stamp

e. Latino parents in Westminster

◆ **FINDING INFORMATION**

Read each question. Find the answer in the paragraph below and circle it. Write the number of the question above your answer.

1. Where was Gonzalo Mendez born?
2. When did he come to the United States?
3. How old was he when he dropped out of school?
4. Why did he drop out of school?
5. What was his wife's name?
6. How many children did they have?
7. What did they own?
8. Where was it?

                                       1.

Gonzalo Mendez was born (in Mexico) and came to the United States when he was a little boy. He dropped out of school at age ten to become a farm worker. He and his wife, Felicitas, had three children and owned a small but successful café in Santa Ana, California.

4. DISCUSSION/WRITING

Imagine this: You are an artist, and you are going to design a postage stamp. Think about important people, places, and things in your community. Which one will you put on the stamp?

In the space below, draw a picture of an important person, place, or thing in your community. Complete the sentences below the picture. Then share your picture and your sentences with a partner.

This is _____. He/She/It is important

because _____.

1. PRE-READING

Look at the picture.

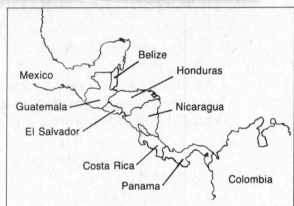

▶ How do you think the men feel?

▶ What do you see in the water?

Look at the map.

▶ Where is Costa Rica?

**Read the title of the story.
Look at the picture again.**

▶ What kind of work do the men do?

▶ What do you think this story is about?

▶ Can you guess what happens?

A Long Fishing Trip

On a warm January morning, Joel Gonzalez kissed his wife goodbye. Joel is a fisherman, and he was going on a short fishing trip. "I'll see you in a week," he said. But Joel did not see his wife in a week. He did not see his wife again for a long, long time.

Joel left his house and went to the harbor in Puntarenas, Costa Rica. He got on a fishing boat. Four other fishermen were on the boat, too. The boat left the harbor, and the men began to fish.

The first few hours on the ocean were not unusual. Then there was a terrible storm. The storm lasted for 22 days. When the storm finally stopped, the men checked their boat. Their fishing nets were gone. The engine and the radio didn't work. There was no food, and there was no fresh water.

For the next few hours, the men talked and planned. "How can we survive on the ocean?" they asked one another. Without their nets, the men couldn't fish. But they could reach out of the boat and catch big turtles. The men didn't want to eat raw turtle meat, so they needed a fire for cooking. They tore down the boat's wood cabin and made a fire with the wood.

They needed protection from the sun and rain, so they built a simple roof. The roof held rainwater, too. The men could drink rainwater from the roof.

For the next five months, the men ate turtles—when they caught them. They drank rainwater—when it rained. Often there was no food and no water, and the men were hungry and thirsty. Sometimes they thought, "We are going to die soon."

Joel wrote a letter to his wife. "My dear Edith," Joel wrote. "If I die, I hope someone will send you this letter. Then you will know how I died. I had the best in life—a great woman and beautiful children. I love you, Edith. I love you."

In June it didn't rain for a long time, and the men ran out of water. They were thin and weak, and they thought, "We are going to die now." They lay down and closed their eyes. After a while, it began to rain. The men stood up and licked the water from the roof. Then all five men began to cry.

Ten days later, on June 15, a Japanese fishing boat found the men. They were 4,000[1] miles from Costa Rica.

Nobody sent Joel's letter to his wife. He showed it to his wife himself. Joel will always keep the letter. The letter, he says, helps him remember. "On the ocean, I realized that I love my wife and children very, very much. My family is everything to me. I don't want to forget that."

[1] 6,437 kilometers

2. VOCABULARY

Complete the sentences with the words below.

~~harbor~~	nets	ran out of	raw	survive

1. Joel went to the _____ *harbor* _____ in Puntarenas. There were many boats there.

2. The fishermen needed their _____ to catch fish.

3. The men didn't want to eat _____ turtle meat, so they built a fire to cook the meat.

4. The men didn't want to die on the ocean; they wanted to _____.

5. The men had nothing to drink because they _____ water.

67

3. COMPREHENSION

♦ **UNDERSTANDING THE MAIN IDEAS**

There are two correct ways to complete each sentence. Circle the letters of the *two* correct answers.

1. Joel Gonzalez
   - **a.** is a fisherman. *(circled)*
   - **b.** is single.
   - **c.** lives in Puntarenas, Costa Rica. *(circled)*

2. After the storm,
   - **a.** there was a hole in the boat.
   - **b.** the boat's engine and radio didn't work.
   - **c.** there was no food or fresh water on the boat.

3. To survive, the men
   - **a.** ate turtle meat.
   - **b.** drank rainwater.
   - **c.** caught birds.

4. In June the men thought they were going to die because they
   - **a.** had no more water.
   - **b.** were all sick.
   - **c.** were thin and weak.

5. When the Japanese fishing boat found the men,
   - **a.** they were 4,000 miles from Costa Rica.
   - **b.** it was five months after the storm.
   - **c.** only three of the fishermen were alive.

♦ **UNDERSTANDING REASONS**

Find the best way to complete each sentence. Write the letter of the answer on the line.

1. The men left Puntarenas __*b*__

2. The men reached out of their boat _____

3. The men tore down the boat's cabin _____

4. Joel wrote his wife a letter _____

5. Joel will keep his letter _____

a. to help him remember that his family is everything to him.

b. to fish on the ocean.

c. to tell her how he died.

d. to catch turtles.

e. to make a fire with the wood.

Imagine this: You want to tell the story "A Long Fishing Trip" to a friend. You want to tell the story quickly, in only four sentences. Which four sentences tell the story best? Check (✓) your answer.

☐ 1. Joel Gonzalez is a Costa Rican fisherman. One January morning, he kissed his wife goodbye and went on a fishing trip. Joel didn't return for five months. While he was away, he wrote his wife a long letter and told her he loved her very much.

☐ 2. Five Costa Rican fishermen were in a terrible storm that lasted for 22 days. After the storm, they were lost at sea for five months. To survive, they ate turtles and drank rainwater. When a Japanese fishing boat found the men, they were 4,000 miles from Costa Rica.

4. DISCUSSION

Fishing is dangerous work. Do you think it is the most dangerous work in the United States?

Read the list of dangerous jobs below. Which job is the most dangerous? In a small group, take a guess. Check (✓) your group's answer. Then tell the class which job your group chose. Were you right? (The answer is in the Answer Key.)

What is the most dangerous job in the United States?

☐ construction worker   ☐ farmer

☐ police officer   ☐ truck driver

☐ pilot   ☐ cashier in a small store

☐ fisherman   ☐ roofer

5. WRITING

Joel wrote a letter to his wife. The end of Joel's letter is missing. Complete Joel's letter on your own paper.

Dear Edith,

If I die, I hope someone will send you this letter. Then you will know how I died. When we left the harbor, everything was fine. Then, a few hours later, there was a terrible storm. It lasted for 22 days. After the storm, we checked our boat. Our fishing nets were . . .

UNIT
18

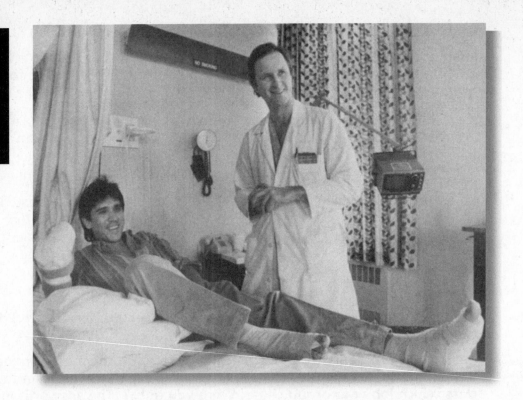

1. PRE-READING

Look at the picture.

▸ Where do you think the men are?

▸ Who is the man in the white coat?

▸ Look at the man on the bed. What does he have on his feet and right hand?

Read the title of the story. Look at the picture again.

▸ What do you think this story is about?

▸ Can you guess what happens?

The Surgeon

On September 19, 1985, Dr. Francisco Bucio was getting dressed for work. His roommate, Angel Alcantara, was combing his hair. Both Francisco and Angel were doctors in Mexico City. They lived and worked together on the fourth floor of General Hospital. Suddenly the hospital began to shake. "Earthquake!" Francisco said. The hospital shook and shook. Then the hospital collapsed. Francisco and Angel fell four floors to the ground below. Three floors of the hospital fell on top of them. The doctors were trapped under a mountain of steel and concrete.

"Angel!" Francisco called to his friend. Angel moaned in pain. Then he was silent. Francisco knew that his friend was dead.

Francisco wanted to cry because Angel was dead. But he told himself, "Keep calm." Then he realized that his right hand was hurt. "Oh, no; oh, no!" Francisco cried. "I can't lose my right hand. My right hand is my future."

For the next four days, Francisco was trapped under the hospital. Every twelve hours, Angel's watch beeped at exactly 7:30. "Angel's watch helped me," Francisco said. "I knew what day it was. But I wondered about my family. Were they safe? And I wondered about Mexico City."

On the third day, Francisco became very thirsty. He dreamed of rivers with no water. He dreamed of ships on dry land.

Then, on the fourth day, rescue workers found Francisco. His right hand was trapped under concrete. The rescue workers wanted to cut off Francisco's hand. "No!" said Francisco.

When rescue workers carried Francisco out of the hospital, he still had his hand. But four fingers were badly crushed. Doctors had to cut off all four fingers on Francisco's right hand. Only his thumb remained. During the next months, Francisco had five operations on his hand. His hand looked better, but it didn't work well. Francisco wanted to be a surgeon. But he needed his right hand to operate on patients.

Then Francisco heard about a surgeon in California who was an expert in hand surgery. Six months after the earthquake, the surgeon operated on Francisco. He cut off two of Francisco's toes and sewed the toes on Francisco's hand. The toes became new fingers for Francisco, and the new fingers worked well.

A year later, Francisco returned to the surgeon in California who had operated on him. He didn't go back as a patient; he went back as a student. Francisco wanted to be an expert surgeon, and his doctor was an expert. Francisco studied with his doctor for three months. Then he returned to Mexico and became a plastic surgeon.

"I know how patients feel," Dr. Bucio said. "I can sympathize and understand. I had six operations, and so much pain—too much pain. Sometimes people joke. They say I'm the surgeon who operates with his feet. OK, my hand isn't beautiful, but I like it. It works."

2. VOCABULARY

Which words have the same meaning as the words in *italics*? Circle the letter of the answer.

1. The hospital *collapsed*.
   a. The hospital disappeared.
   b. The hospital fell down.
2. The doctors were *trapped* under a mountain of steel and concrete.
   a. A mountain of steel and concrete was on top of the doctors. They couldn't move.
   b. The doctors climbed a mountain of steel and concrete.

3. Angel *moaned* in pain.
   a. Angel made a sound because he was in pain.
   b. Angel closed his eyes because he was in pain.
4. "I know how patients feel," Dr. Bucio said. "I can *sympathize* and understand."
   a. "I understand patients' feelings and pain because I, too, had a lot of pain."
   b. "My patients are kind people, and I like them very much."

71

3. COMPREHENSION

◆ **UNDERSTANDING THE MAIN IDEAS**

There are two correct ways to complete each sentence. Circle the letters of the *two* correct answers.

1. On September 19, 1985,

    a. there was an earthquake in Mexico City.

    b. Francisco Bucio was a patient in a hospital.

    c. General Hospital in Mexico City collapsed.

2. During the four days Francisco was trapped under the hospital, he

    a. talked to his friend.

    b. wondered about his family.

    c. became very thirsty.

3. When rescue workers carried Francisco out of the hospital,

    a. he still had both hands.

    b. the fingers on his right hand were badly crushed.

    c. his right leg was broken.

4. The surgeon who was an expert in hand surgery

    a. cut off two of Francisco's toes.

    b. sewed the toes on Francisco's right hand.

    c. worked at General Hospital in Mexico City.

5. Today Francisco Bucio

    a. lives in the United States.

    b. is a plastic surgeon.

    c. knows how his patients feel.

◆ **UNDERSTANDING TIME RELATIONSHIPS**

Find the best way to complete each sentence. Write the letter of the answer on the line.

1. On September 19, 1985, __*e*__   **a.** rescue workers found Francisco.

2. Every twelve hours, _____   **b.** an expert in hand surgery operated on Francisco.

3. On the third day, _____

4. On the fourth day, _____   **c.** Francisco became very thirsty.

5. Six months after the earthquake, _____   **d.** Angel's watch beeped.

    e. there was an earthquake in Mexico City.

Imagine this: You want to tell the story "The Surgeon" to a friend. You want to tell the story quickly, in only five sentences. Which five sentences tell the story best? Check (✓) your answer.

☐ **1.** A hospital in Mexico City collapsed during an earthquake. One of the doctors was trapped under the hospital for four days. He was rescued, but the fingers on his right hand were badly crushed, and doctors had to cut them off. Later, an expert in hand surgery cut off two of the doctor's toes and sewed the toes on the doctor's right hand. The doctor is now a surgeon and operates on patients.

☐ **2.** In 1985 there was an earthquake in Mexico City, and a hospital collapsed. A doctor who lived and worked in the hospital fell four floors to the ground below. Three floors of the hospital fell on top of him, and he was trapped under a mountain of steel and concrete. During his four days under the hospital, the doctor worried about his right hand. He also worried about his family and about Mexico City.

4. DISCUSSION/WRITING

On September 19, 1985, there was an earthquake in Mexico. An earthquake is a natural disaster.

A. On the map below, look at the places where natural disasters sometimes happen in the United States. Discuss new vocabulary with your classmates.

B. On your own paper, draw a map of your native country. Mark the places where natural disasters sometimes happen. Then, show your map to a partner. Tell your partner about natural disasters in your native country. Finally, on your own paper, write about a natural disaster that happened in your native country. Or, write about a natural disaster that *you* experienced.

1. PRE-READING

Look at the picture.

▸ How old is the woman?

▸ How does she feel?

▸ What is she going to do with the hammer?

Read the title of the story. Look at the picture again.

▸ What do you think this story is about?

▸ Can you guess what happens?

Customer Service?

Mona Shaw is a quiet grandmother who lives a quiet life in a quiet suburb of Washington, D.C. But one afternoon Mona made a lot of noise with a hammer. She didn't make noise because she was building something or fixing something. She made a lot of noise because she was angry.

Mona's troubles began when she got a letter from a big telephone company. "Sign up now for our special offer," the letter said. "We'll give you three services—telephone, TV service, and high-speed Internet—for only $100 a month." That seemed like a good deal, so Mona called the company. "I'd like to sign up for your special offer," she said.

"Great!" a company representative said. "A technician will be at your house on Monday."

Mona stayed home all day on Monday. The technician didn't come.

On Wednesday the technician finally came. First, he disconnected Mona's old telephone service. Then he tried to connect the new telephone service. But he had a problem, and he couldn't finish the job. "I'll come back tomorrow," he said.

The technician didn't come back. Now Mona had a problem: She had no telephone service. She was worried. She was 75 years old, and she had a bad heart. "What if I need to call 911 for help?" Mona thought. She went to the company's office.

"May I help you?" a smiling customer service representative asked Mona.

"A technician came to my house and disconnected my old phone service, but he couldn't connect the new service," Mona said. "Can someone come as soon as possible to finish the job?"

"You need to talk to the manager," the customer service representative said. "Please take a seat."

Mona sat down and waited . . . and waited . . . and waited . . . and waited. Two hours later, the customer service representative told her, "I'm really sorry. The manager went home. You'll have to come back another day."

Mona went to a neighbor's house and called the company. "Someone will come to your house next Tuesday," a company representative said.

Mona waited all day Tuesday. Nobody came. At 4:30 that afternoon, Mona went down to the basement, got her husband's hammer, and went back to the company's office. She walked over to the customer service representative's computer. BAM! She hit the computer's monitor with the hammer. BAM! She hit the keyboard. BAM! She hit the telephone that was next to the computer.

"I don't have telephone service," she told the customer service representative. "Now you don't, either." BAM! She hit the phone again.

A few minutes later, the police arrived and arrested Mona. Later, a judge told Mona, "You have to pay $345 for the damage to the computer and the phone." That was okay with Mona. "I don't mind paying the money," she said. "It was worth it. I feel *so* much better."

Mona has good telephone service now. It is with a different company.

2. VOCABULARY

Complete the sentences with the words below.

damage	don't mind	~~good deal~~	What if

1. Telephone, TV, and Internet service can cost $200 a month or more. But one company was giving the three services for only $100 a month. That was a ____*good deal*____.

2. Mona was thinking about the future. "Maybe I'll have a problem with my heart," she thought. _____ I need to call 911?"

3. Mona broke a lot of things at the company's office. She had to pay $345 for the _____.

4. Mona had to pay $345, but that was okay with her. "I _____ paying the money," she said.

3. COMPREHENSION

◆ **UNDERSTANDING THE MAIN IDEAS**

Circle the letter of the best answer.

1. This is a story about a woman who
   a. is good at building and fixing things.
   b. had trouble with her computer.
   c. got very angry at a company.

2. The woman went to the company's office and
   a. hit things with a hammer.
   b. told the manager, "I'm never coming here again."
   c. talked to a customer service representative for an hour.

3. Now the woman says she feels
   a. sorry for what she did.
   b. much better.
   c. angry at her husband.

◆ **REMEMBERING DETAILS**

1. **Which sentences describe Mona? Check (✓) six answers. (The first one is done for you.)**

   ☑ She is a grandmother.
   ☐ She usually lives a quiet life.
   ☐ She lives in a suburb of Washington, D.C.
   ☐ She works for a telephone company.
   ☐ She is 75 years old.
   ☐ She has trouble walking.
   ☐ She has a bad heart.
   ☐ She is married.

2. **Why was Mona angry with the telephone company?**
Check (✓) four answers.

☐ On Monday she waited all day for the technician, but he didn't come.

☐ The technician disconnected her old phone service, but he couldn't connect her new service.

☐ The company said its special offer cost $100, but it cost $300.

☐ Mona waited for two hours to talk to the manager.

☐ The company's office was open only two hours a day.

☐ A company representative told Mona, "Someone will come to your house next Tuesday," but nobody came.

◆ **UNDERSTANDING WORD GROUPS**

Read each group of words. One word in each group doesn't belong. Find the word and cross it out.

technician	computer	hammer	police
~~nurse~~	lamp	build	teacher
customer service representative	monitor	fix	arrest
company representative	keyboard	cook	judge

4. DISCUSSION/WRITING

A. In your native country, what do you do if you have a problem with something you bought—if, for example, it is broken or doesn't work? Tell the class.

B. Have you ever had a bad experience with a company? Tell the class about it.

C. What can you do if you have a problem with a company? In a small group, make a list of things you can do. On the lines below, write your ideas. Then share them with the class.

_____

_____

_____

1. PRE-READING

Look at the picture.

▸ How old do you think the girl is?

▸ What pictures do you see on the balloon?

Read the title of the story. Look at the picture again.

▸ What do you think this story is about?

▸ Can you guess what happens?

The Mermaid Balloon

"Grandma!" little Desiree exclaimed. "It's my daddy's birthday. How will I send him a birthday card?"

Desiree's grandmother looked at Desiree and sighed. She didn't know what to say. Desiree's father had died nine months earlier. Desiree didn't understand. She was only four years old.

"I have an idea," her grandmother said. "Let's write your daddy a letter. We can tie the letter to a balloon and send it up to heaven. What should we write?"

Desiree told her grandmother to write, "Happy Birthday, Daddy. I love you and miss you. Please write me on my birthday in January."

Desiree's grandmother wrote Desiree's message and their address on a small piece of paper. Then Desiree, her mother, and her grandmother went to a store to buy a balloon. Desiree looked quickly at the helium-filled balloons and said, "That one! The one with the mermaid!"

They bought the mermaid balloon and tied Desiree's letter to it. Then Desiree let the balloon go. For an hour, they watched the balloon go higher and higher. Finally, it disappeared. "Did you see that?" Desiree exclaimed. "Daddy reached down and took my balloon! Now he's going to write me back!"

Desiree released the balloon in California. The wind caught the balloon and carried it east. Four days later, it came down 3,000 miles away, near a lake in eastern Canada. The name of the lake was Mermaid Lake.

Wade MacKinnon, a Canadian man, was hunting ducks at Mermaid Lake when he found Desiree's balloon and letter. He took them home to his wife.

She decided to send Desiree a birthday present. She also wrote her a letter. The letter said:

Dear Desiree,
Happy Birthday from your daddy. I guess you wonder who we are. Well, my husband, Wade, went duck hunting, and guess what he found! A mermaid balloon that you sent your daddy. There are no stores in heaven, so your daddy wanted someone to do his shopping for him. I think he picked us because we live in a town called Mermaid. I know your daddy loves you very much and will always watch over you.
Lots of love,
The MacKinnons

When the package from the MacKinnons arrived, Desiree was not at all surprised. "Daddy remembered my birthday!" she exclaimed.

Desiree's mother wrote the MacKinnons to thank them for the present and the letter. During the next few weeks, she and the MacKinnons telephoned each other often. Then Desiree, her mother, and her grandmother flew to Canada to meet the MacKinnons. The MacKinnons took them to Mermaid Lake and showed them where the balloon had landed.

Now, whenever Desiree wants to talk about her father, she calls the MacKinnons. After she talks to them, she feels better.

People often say, "What a coincidence—the mermaid balloon landed at Mermaid Lake!" Desiree's mother is not sure it was just a coincidence. She says, "I think that somehow my husband picked the MacKinnons. It was his way to send his love to Desiree. She understands now that her father is with her always."

2. VOCABULARY

Which words have the same meaning as the words in *italics*? Circle the letter of the answer.

1. "Grandma!" Desiree *exclaimed*. "It's my daddy's birthday!"
   a. said suddenly, with strong feeling
   b. said slowly, with a very quiet voice
2. Desiree *released* the balloon.
   a. opened her eyes and looked at the balloon
   b. opened her hand and let the balloon go

3. Wade MacKinnon was *hunting* ducks.
   a. trying to shoot
   b. trying to paint
4. Desiree's mother thinks her husband *picked* the MacKinnons to send his love to Desiree.
   a. chose
   b. paid

3. COMPREHENSION

◆ **UNDERSTANDING THE MAIN IDEA**

Circle the letter of your answer.

1. What was the coincidence in the story?
   a. Desiree and her father have the same birthday, January 12.
   b. The mermaid balloon came down at Mermaid Lake.
   c. The MacKinnons also have a four-year-old daughter.
2. Desiree feels better now because
   a. she got a lot of presents for her birthday.
   b. she can talk to the MacKinnons about her father.
   c. she spends a lot of time with her grandmother.

◆ **REMEMBERING DETAILS**

One word in each sentence is not correct. Find the word and cross it out. Write the correct word.

1. Desiree tied a ~~present~~ *letter* to a helium-filled balloon.

2. The balloon had a picture of a fish on it.

3. Desiree released the balloon in Arizona.

4. The wind carried the balloon south.

5. Four years later, the balloon came down 3,000 miles away.

6. The balloon landed near a mountain in eastern Canada.

7. A Canadian man was feeding ducks when he found Desiree's letter.

8. The MacKinnons decided to send Desiree a birthday cake and a letter.

◆ **FINDING MORE INFORMATION**

Read each sentence on the left. Which sentence on the right gives you more information? Write the letter of the answer on the line.

___b___ 1. Desiree wrote her father a letter.

_____ 2. Desiree chose a balloon at the store.

_____ 3. The balloon came down near a lake.

_____ 4. A Canadian man found the balloon.

a. It was in eastern Canada, and its name was Mermaid Lake.

b. It said, "Please write me on my birthday in January."

c. It was filled with helium, and it had a picture of a mermaid on it.

d. His name was Wade MacKinnon, and he was hunting ducks.

4. DISCUSSION

The mermaid balloon landed at Mermaid Lake. That was a coincidence. Can you find any coincidences among your classmates?

Complete the sentences. (Skip the sentences you can't complete.)

1. My birthday is _____ _____.
                       (month)   (day)

2. Once I broke a bone in my _____.

3. Last summer I took a trip to _____.

4. A car I like is _____.

5. I like to play _____.

6. Last night I dreamed about _____.

In a small group, take turns reading your sentences. Did any students complete a sentence in the same way? Tell the class about any coincidences you discovered.

5. WRITING

Write a letter on your own paper. Put your letter in a small plastic bag. Tie your letter to a helium-filled balloon and let the balloon go. Here is what one student wrote.

My name is Andrea. I am a student at the American Language Institute in Indiana, PA. If you find my letter, please write me and tell me how far my balloon went. My address is:

American Language Institute
Eicher Hall
Indiana University of Pennsylvania
Indiana, PA 15705

One more thing: I am from Slovakia, but I speak English.

1. PRE-READING

Look at the picture.

▸ How old do you think the woman is?

▸ Who do you think the child is?

▸ Can you guess when the woman lived?

Read the title of the story. Look at the picture again.

▸ What do you think this story is about?

▸ Can you guess what happens?

The Two Lives of Mary Sutton

Do you believe in reincarnation—that you lived before? Jenny Cockell does. Jenny is a doctor who lives in England. She is married and has two children. That is Jenny's present life. Jenny believes that she also had a past life. She believes she was Mary Sutton, an Irish woman who died in 1932.

When Jenny was four years old, she began dreaming about a woman named Mary. She had the same dreams again and again. In one dream, the woman was standing on a beach and looking at the ocean. She seemed to be waiting for someone. In one terrible dream, the woman was lying in bed in a white room. She was dying.

Sometimes in her dreams Jenny saw the woman's village. Jenny thought that it was on the coast of Ireland. Often she looked at a map of Ireland and read the names of villages on the coast. One name—Malahide—seemed familiar. Jenny thought that maybe Malahide was the woman's village.

Jenny dreamed about Mary and Mary's village all her life. Finally, when she was 36 years old, she decided to travel to Ireland. She wanted to see Malahide.

When Jenny arrived in Malahide, she knew immediately that it was the village in her dreams. The streets, the shops, and the churches all looked familiar. She was in Mary's village!

Jenny decided to look for Mary's little house. She had seen it often in her dreams. It was on a narrow road south of the village. Jenny walked to the south end of the village and found a narrow road. She walked down the road, but there was no house. There was only an old barn.

When Jenny got back to England, she wrote a letter to the man who owned the barn. "Was there ever a small house near your barn?" she asked him.

"Yes," the man wrote back. "There was once a small house near the barn. A family with six children lived there. The mother died in childbirth in 1932. Her name was Mary Sutton."

Jenny found out that after Mary died, Mary's husband couldn't take care of their children. He gave them to other people, and they grew up apart. Jenny decided to find Mary's children. Two of the six children had died, but Jenny found the four surviving children. "Please meet me in Malahide," Jenny wrote them.

In Malahide, Mary's children, who were in their sixties and seventies, told Jenny stories about their childhood.

Sonny, the oldest child, said, "When I was 12, I got a job on an island near Malahide. Every evening a boat brought me home. My mother often waited for me on the beach."

All of the stories seemed familiar to Jenny; she is sure that she is the reincarnation of Mary Sutton. Some of the Sutton children think so, too. Sonny, who is 35 years older than Jenny, says, "To me, she is my mother."

2. VOCABULARY

Complete the sentences with the words below.

barn	childhood	surviving	~~village~~

1. Only a few hundred people live in Malahide. It is a _____*village*_____.

2. Jenny walked down a narrow road south of the village, but she saw no house. She saw only a building where animals sleep. She saw a _____.

3. Two of Mary's six children had died, but Jenny found the four children who were alive. She found the _____ children.

4. The Sutton children told Jenny about the time when they were children in Malahide. They told stories about their _____.

3. COMPREHENSION

◆ **UNDERSTANDING THE MAIN IDEA**

Circle the letter of the best answer.

1. Jenny believes she is the reincarnation of Mary Sutton because

    a. Mary Sutton was her grandmother.

    b. she saw Mary's life in her dreams.

    c. most people in England believe in reincarnation.

2. Jenny's dreams gave her a lot of information about Mary's life. All of the information was

    a. wonderful.

    b. sad.

    c. correct.

◆ **FINDING MORE INFORMATION**

Read each sentence on the left. Which sentence on the right gives you more information? Write the letter of the answer on the line.

___e___ **1.** Jenny Cockell has a present life.	**a.** It was on the coast of Ireland, and its name was Malahide.
_____ **2.** Jenny believes she also had a past life.	**b.** She believes she was Mary Sutton, an Irish woman who died in 1932.
_____ **3.** Jenny had the same dreams again and again.	**c.** In one dream, a woman was standing on a beach.
_____ **4.** In her dreams, Jenny saw the woman's village.	**d.** It was on a narrow road south of the village.
_____ **5.** Jenny looked for Mary's house.	**e.** She is a doctor who lives in England.
_____ **6.** Jenny looked for Mary's children.	**f.** They were in their 60s and 70s.

◆ **REMEMBERING DETAILS**

Read each sentence. If the sentence describes Jenny Cockell, write a _J_ for Jenny. If the sentence describes Mary Sutton, write an _M_ for Mary.

___J___ **1.** She lives in England.	_____ **5.** She has two children.
_____ **2.** She lived in Ireland.	_____ **6.** Her son worked on an island.
_____ **3.** She had six children.	_____ **7.** She dreamed about a woman.
_____ **4.** She often looked at maps of Ireland.	_____ **8.** She lived in a little house on a narrow road.

4. DISCUSSION

When she was a child, Jenny drew a map of the village she saw in her dreams. Look at the map that Jenny drew. Then look at an actual map of Malahide, Ireland.

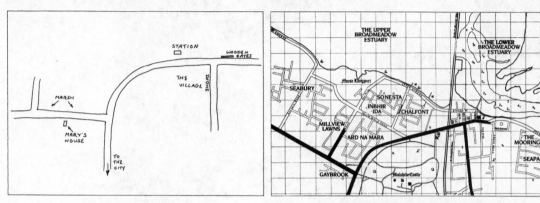

Jenny's Map   Actual Map of Malahide, Ireland

Think about the story and the two maps. Then read the questions and check (✓) your answers. Explain your answers in a small group.

1. Do you believe that Jenny Cockell is the reincarnation of Mary Sutton?
   ☐ Yes
   ☐ No
   ☐ Maybe

2. Do you believe that you have a past life—that you lived before?
   ☐ Yes
   ☐ No
   ☐ Maybe

5. WRITING

When Jenny was in Malahide, she kept a diary. She wrote down everything she saw and did.

Complete Jenny's diary on your own paper.

> *June 3*
>
> *When I arrived in Malahide, I went to a small hotel in the center of the village. After I unpacked my suitcase, I ate lunch at the hotel. Then I went outside to look around the village . . .*

1. PRE-READING

Look at the picture.

▶ Where does the man live?

▶ How does he feel?

▶ Who are the two girls?

**Read the title of the story.
Look at the drawing on this page.**

▶ Where do you think the two
strangers met?

▶ What do you think this story
is about?

▶ Can you guess what happens?

PLATFORM

Two Strangers

One afternoon Wesley Autrey and his two young daughters, ages four and six, were standing on a subway platform in New York City. Wesley was a construction worker on the second shift. He was taking his daughters home from school before he went to work.

A young man was standing nearby. He was Cameron Peters, a 20-year-old student. Suddenly Cameron began to shake all over and fell to the ground. He had epilepsy, and he was having a seizure. Wesley knew first aid, so he ran to help Cameron. He put a pen between Cameron's teeth so he wouldn't bite his tongue. Then he waited for Cameron to stop shaking. When the seizure was over, Cameron stood up. "Are you all right?" Wesley asked him. "Yes, I'm fine," Cameron answered.

Wesley was walking away when Cameron had another seizure. He fell to the ground again, but this time he fell off the subway platform and onto the tracks below. Wesley looked into the tunnel at the end of the station and saw two white lights. A train was coming. "Hold on to my daughters," Wesley yelled to two women who were standing on the platform. Then he jumped down onto the tracks.

Wesley tried to lift Cameron and put him back on the platform, but he couldn't. Cameron was heavier than he was, and the platform was four feet above the tracks. Wesley looked into the tunnel again. The two white lights were much closer now. The train was coming into the station.

Wesley looked down and saw that there was a space between the tracks about 22 inches deep. As a construction worker, Wesley often worked in small spaces. "I think we can both fit," he decided. He pushed Cameron into the space between the tracks. Then he lay down on top of him. "Don't move," Wesley said, "or one of us is going to lose a leg."

The driver of the train saw the two men on the tracks and put on the brakes. But he wasn't able to stop the train in time. When the first car of the train went over Wesley and Cameron, it moved Wesley's hat a little. Wesley put his head down further, and four more cars went over them. When the train stopped, Wesley and Cameron were under the fifth car. Wesley could hear people on the platform screaming. "We're okay down here," he yelled, "but I've got two daughters up there. Let them know their father's okay."

Paramedics arrived and helped Wesley and Cameron out from under the train. They were both fine.

Cameron remembers almost nothing about the experience. He doesn't remember falling off the platform, and he doesn't remember the train going over him and Wesley. He remembers waking up after the train stopped and seeing Wesley's face. "Am I dead?" he asked Wesley. "Am I in heaven?"

"No, you're not dead, and you're not in heaven," Wesley answered. "You're alive, and you're under a subway train in New York City."

"Who are you?" Cameron asked, and Wesley answered, "I'm someone who saved your life."

2. VOCABULARY

Which words have the same meaning as the words in italics? Write the letter of the answer on the line.

___b___ **1.** Wesley worked from *three o'clock in the afternoon to eleven o'clock at night*.

_____ **2.** Wesley knew how to give *emergency medical help*.

_____ **3.** The driver *couldn't* stop the train.

_____ **4.** "*Tell them* their father's okay."

_____ **5.** Wesley asked Cameron, "Are you *okay*?"

a. Let them know

b. the second shift

c. first aid

d. all right

e. wasn't able to

3. COMPREHENSION

◆ **UNDERSTANDING THE MAIN IDEAS**

Complete the sentences. Write your answers on the lines.

1. Wesley and Cameron were standing on a ____*subway*____ ____*platform*____.

2. When Cameron had the second seizure, he _____ off the platform and onto the _____ below.

3. Wesley looked into the tunnel and saw two white _____.

4. Wesley couldn't put Cameron back on the platform because Cameron was _____ than he was, and the platform was four _____ above the tracks.

5. Wesley pushed Cameron into the space _____ the _____.

6. When the first car went over the two men, it moved Wesley's _____ a little.

7. When the train stopped, the men were under the _____ car.

8. From under the train, Wesley yelled, "Let _____ know their father's okay."

◆ **UNDERSTANDING TIME RELATIONSHIPS**

Find the best way to complete each sentence. Write the letter of the answer on the line.

1. Wesley was walking away __*b*__

2. The driver of the train put on the breaks _____

3. Wesley put his head down further _____

4. "We're okay down here," Wesley yelled _____

5. "Am I dead?" Cameron asked Wesley _____

a. when he woke up under the train.

b. when Cameron had another seizure.

c. when he heard people on the platform screaming.

d. when the first car moved his hat a little.

e. when he saw the two men on the tracks.

◆ **FINDING INFORMATION**

Read each question. Find the answer in the paragraphs below and circle it. Write the number of the question above your answer.

1. What is Wesley's last name?
2. How old were his daughters?
3. In what city is the subway platform?
4. What was Wesley's work?
5. When did he work?
6. Where was he taking his daughters?

   One afternoon Wesley Autrey and his two young daughters, ages four and six, were standing on a subway platform in New York City. Wesley was a construction worker on the second shift. He was taking his daughters home from school before he went to work.

4. DISCUSSION/WRITING

Many people admire Wesley Autrey: They like him and have a good opinion of him. We admire someone who saves another person's life—especially if the other person is a stranger. What kind of person do *you* admire?

A. Think of three ways to complete the sentence below. Write your answers on the lines. Then share your answers with the class.

I admire someone who . . .

_____ .

_____ .

_____ .

B. On your own paper, write a paragraph about someone you admire. Explain why you admire him or her. Here is what one student wrote.

> *I admire my mother because she is a strong woman. My father died when I was four years old, and my mother took care of ten children alone.*

To the Teacher

The original newspaper and magazine versions of these TRUE STORIES contain information that could not be included in the adaptations. Sometimes the information was too complicated to include; sometimes including it would have made the stories too long for the allotted space. On the other hand, the information—in many cases, the story behind the story—was just too interesting to leave out entirely. So, it was decided that additional facts and updates would be given here, in a special "To the Teacher" section.

As you will see from the sophistication of the language, this section is not meant for students. You might want to offer the information only if students seem puzzled or curious, or if, in the context of the class discussion, the information would be particularly meaningful.

Also included here are supplemental reading and vocabulary activities, all of them no-prep, as well as specific teaching tips for the discussion and writing exercises.

All Units

Before Reading

A. Illustrate the story.

If your students need extra support, you might want to tell them the story before they read it, stopping well short of the ending. As you tell the story, draw pictures on the board to illustrate it. Following are some tips for drawing.

1. Keep it simple! To draw a person, most of the time just drawing the head and shoulders suffices—no need to draw arms, legs, feet, ears. Add a few squiggles to represent hair if the person is female. Smaller heads and shoulders are children. Add two dots for the eyes, a dot for the nose, and a line for the mouth, and the figure is complete. For example, the figures might look something like these:

2. Use the same symbols consistently to represent the same things so that students get used to your drawing style. For example, two parallel lines with a triangle-shaped roof (resembling a child's drawing of a house) represent a building. A dollar sign inside means the building is a bank; a shopping cart indicates it is a supermarket.

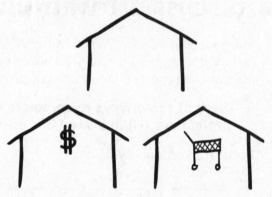

3. Draw nouns to represent verbs. For example, draw a knife to represent "to cut."

4. Feel free to move back and forth between drawing images from the story and acting out scenes. You could even pretend to take hold of items you drew on the board (such as a balloon) and use them as props in your reenactment of a scene. Or you could interact with objects you drew. For example, you could knock on a picture of a door.

Drawing tips 1–3 are the suggestions of Norma Shapiro, whose reference book *Chalk Talks* (Command Performance Language Institute, 1994) has further tips and hundreds of examples of simple drawings.

B. Invent a story.

Instead of telling students the actual story, you can guide them into fabricating an alternate version of it by asking questions and encouraging students to guess the answers. Here, for example, is how a pre-reading question-and-answer session for the story "Customer Service?" (Unit 19) might play out:

Teacher (pointing to photo):
What's her name?

Student: Her name is Mary.

Teacher: OK, her name is Mary. What's her last name?

Student: Her last name is Carter.

Teacher: OK, her last name is Carter. How old is she?

Student: She's 70 years old.

Teacher: OK, she's 70 years old. Where does she live?

Student: She lives in Chicago.

Teacher: Does she live in the city or in a suburb?

Student: She lives in the city.

Teacher: OK, she lives in Chicago, in the city. What is she going to do with the hammer?

Students: She's going to fix something. / Robbers are in her house, and she's going to hit them with it. / She's a carpenter, and she's going to build something.

Teacher: OK, let's say robbers are in her house. What do they want to take?

Student: They want to take her computer and her TV.

Teacher: What happens? Does she hit the robbers with the hammer?

Student: No, they see the hammer and they run away.

Teacher: (*At this point, the teacher recounts the fabricated story.*)
OK, that's *our* story. Now let's read the *true* story.

Students can answer the questions orally, with volunteers guessing answers, or they can write their answers and then read them to a partner. If you choose to make this activity a whole-class effort, you can illustrate the students' answers with simple drawings on the board. (Please see the drawing tips above.) After reading, you can go back to the illustrations of the fabricated story and contrast the guessed answers with the actual facts. ("We said her name was Mary, but her name is . . . .")

C. Discuss first.

If you think students might have had experiences similar to those in the story, you could have them complete the discussion exercise before, rather than after, they read. For example, before reading "Customer Service?" (Unit 19), you could tell students that the story is about a woman who had a bad experience with a company and then ask them if they have had any bad experiences with a company—if, for example, they bought a cell-phone plan that was more expensive than they expected it to be or if they bought something that they were unable to return.

D. Describe the photo.

Prompt students to describe the photo by saying, "Look at the picture. What do you see?" Sometimes students respond more readily to the general question "What do you see?" than to a more specific question, such as "Who do you think these people are?" When asked a specific question, some students are reluctant to speak; they assume there is a specific correct answer. When asked "What do you see?" they are more inclined to respond because it is clearer that any reasonable answer is acceptable.

E. Pose pre-reading questions.

If your students are comfortable speaking English, you may wish to guide them into posing their own pre-reading questions. After the class describes the photo and reads the title of the story, ask, "What do you want to know?" Write the students' questions on the board. Return to the questions after reading the story to see which were answered.

F. Ask illogical pre-reading questions.

For example, before reading Unit 10, "Please Pass the Bird Brains," ask students, "Is the man in the photo from Mexico? Is he a mechanic? Does he work in a garage? Are there toys on the shelves behind the man?" When the students respond, "No," they will naturally supply answers that are more logical. The questions can also be phrased as statements, for example, "The man in the photo is from Mexico, right?"

During Reading

A. Read aloud.

If your students understand spoken English well but have little experience reading, you may wish to begin by reading the story aloud or playing the recording of the story, perhaps stopping short of the last few paragraphs if the story has a surprise ending.

B. Predict the text.

If you are reading the story aloud to students, pause occasionally and ask them, "What will happen next?"

C. Read twice.

Students who have a tendency to stop at every unknown word should be encouraged to read the story twice, once without stopping to get the gist of the story, and then a second time, stopping to underline new vocabulary.

After Reading

A. Read with mistakes.

Read the story (or a section of the story) aloud, making mistakes as you read. For example, you could begin the story "Two Strangers" (Unit 22) this way: "One *morning* Wesley Autrey and his two young *sons,* ages four and six, were standing on a subway platform in *Boston.*" Students call out the errors.

B. Whisper read.

Read the story aloud. Students read along with you, mouthing the words inaudibly and trying to keep up with your pace.

C. Fill in the blanks.

This is an oral cloze activity. Read the story aloud as students follow along in their textbooks. Stop periodically and look up expectantly. Students provide the word that comes next.

D. Stand up when you hear your word.

Write key words from the story on index cards and pass the cards out to selected students. Read the story aloud. Students stand up when they hear the words on their cards. (Because students are continually standing up and sitting down, this is sometimes called a "popcorn" activity. It is especially suitable for young learners.)

E. Rewrite the story.

If students have solid writing skills, they can rewrite the story from a different point of view. For example, the story "Two Strangers" (Unit 22) could be told by one of the women on the platform or by Wesley Autrey as a first-person account.

F. Role-play.

Students write a short skit based on the story and then act out their roles in front of the class. For example, students could role-play the conversation between Selma and Maria when Selma brings her baby to Maria's house (Unit 5) or the conversation between John and his doctor when John finds out he is not going to die (Unit 3).

G. Write a walking dictation.

Many units have a "Remembering Details" exercise in which students find the incorrect word in each sentence, cross it out, and write the correct word. These sentences can be the basis of a "walking dictation." Students place their books on the opposite side of the room. They memorize the first sentence, "carry" it back to their desks, and write it down. They continue walking back and forth until they have copied all the sentences. Then they take their seats, find the incorrect word in each sentence, cross it out, and write the correct word.

H. Write a disappearing summary.

Students, working as a class, summarize the story. (Stipulate that the summary should consist of four or five sentences.) Write their summary on the board, correcting errors as you write or after the summary is complete. Read the first sentence of the summary; students repeat in unison. Erase a word or two of the sentence and say it again; students repeat in unison. Continue erasing words a few at a time. After each erasure, say the sentence and ask students to repeat. Ultimately, students will be saying a sentence that has been totally erased. Repeat the process with the remaining sentences. When all the sentences have been erased, ask students to recite the summary from memory.

I. Write true/false sentences.

1. Write three sentences on the board as a model. Explain that two sentences are true, and one sentence is false. Ask students to identify the sentence that is false. You could, for example, write three sentences about your classroom:

   This is Room 131.
   There are 28 desks in this room.
   The walls are yellow.

2. Students write three sentences (two true and one false) about the story. When they are finished writing, they give their sentences to a partner. The partner reads the sentences and crosses out the sentence that is false. To narrow the task, have students write true/false sentences about specific people and topics in the story. For example, for the story "The School and the Stamp" (Unit 16), they could write three sentences about the stamp, Gonzalo Mendez, or the "Mexican school."

All Units

Vocabulary

Research indicates that students' retention of new vocabulary depends not so much on the type of vocabulary exercises they complete but on how much exposure they have to the new words. The more times they "touch" a word, the more likely it is they will remember it. So you will probably want to follow up the exercises in the text with supplemental activities, such as writing the words on flash cards and presenting them again in subsequent classes. Similarly, research shows that the particular method students use to learn vocabulary—whether they write the new words on small flash cards, for example, or in a vocabulary notebook—is not as important as simply having a system for memorizing vocabulary. To promote the use of such systems, present several strategies for learning new words and encourage students to share their own techniques. Knowledge of vocabulary is a key component of reading comprehension, so it is important to devise a system for learning new words in class and to encourage students to devise their own systems for learning words at home. If your students are employed adults who have little time to study outside of class, it is particularly important to devote some class time to vocabulary study, either before or after reading.

A. Roxie Daggett, ESL specialist at Santa Fe (NM) Community College, shares this innovative pre-reading activity:

Before we read the story, we practice vocabulary I anticipate will be tricky to understand or pronounce. (Or you can have the students select the vocabulary after a first reading.) First, I write the vocabulary on the board and draw pictures or write simple definitions that the class and I come up with together. For example, for the word *search* (Unit 6), I might write this definition: "to look for." Then comes the fun part. We stand in a circle and create gestures that go with each word. We read the word and definition aloud together. Then I ask for a gesture, and they come up with one. (For the word *search*, students might shade their eyes with one hand, palm down, and scan the room.) Then we practice: I say the word, and they do the gesture; then I do the gesture, and they say the word. Finally, they practice with partners so that I can check their understanding individually as one student says words and the other gestures. Sometimes I have them create gestures as teams and quiz the other team. Once, during team charades, a whole team collapsed on their desks to model the word *faint* (Unit 5). I learned much of this from a colleague who believes in engaging the whole body, including the sense of humor, in language acquisition.

B. The following is another effective, no-prep activity, this one for reviewing vocabulary after reading:

1. Select 8–10 words from the story and, at the end of class or in a subsequent class, write them on the board in random order, perhaps scattering the words across the board.

2. Choose a word and orally describe a situation in which it could be used, but do not say the word. For example, if the target word is *refund*, from Unit 15, you might say, "Lillian paid too much money to the government for taxes. So the government sent her a _____ of $462." (Replace the word with a spoken "beep.") The context can be from the story or it can be a new context, for example: "My sister gave me a size medium sweater for my birthday, but it was too small. I went to the store to exchange it for a size large, but they didn't have a size large. So I gave the saleswoman the sweater and the receipt, and she gave me a _____." After students call out the target word, draw a line through it.

Continue giving examples and drawing lines through the remaining words.

3. When students become comfortable with the activity, student volunteers can take turns giving examples of the target words in context. (You will need to remind them not to say the target words.) Initially they might balk, but with time they will become skilled at giving examples, sometimes from their own lives.

A game called Flyswatter Vocabulary, appropriate for young learners, is a variation of this activity. Increase the number of vocabulary items on the board to 12–15. Students line up in two teams facing the board, about six feet from it. The students at the front of each line have flyswatters. Orally describe a situation in which one of the words on the board could be used, but do not say the word. The first person to swat the target word with the flyswatter wins a point for his/her team. After each word, the two students with the flyswatters hand the flyswatters to the person behind them and go to the end of the line.

Unit 1   Puppy Love

An Okinawa newspaper, the *Ryuku Shimpo*, reported that Marilyn and Shiro became the parents of six puppies. Marilyn's owners received requests for a puppy from people all over Japan.

Shiro's pedigree is described as "mutt." The Nakamuras found him in the garbage when he was a puppy.

Unit 2   Surprise! It's Your Wedding!

After the wedding, John said of Lynn, "She's great fun to be with and often does practical jokes, but I didn't think she'd dare do anything like this."

It is not known if Lynn and John lived happily ever after.

Unit 3 Bad News, Good News

The initial tests at the hospital indicated that John had a three-inch tumor on his pancreas. A subsequent biopsy revealed no cancer, but doctors attributed those results to a "sampling error" and held to their original diagnosis of terminal cancer. They now believe that the "tumor" was probably a swelling rather than a malignancy and that the diagnosis should have been pancreatitis—inflammation of the pancreas. John faults the doctors at the hospital for not doing more tests after the biopsy was negative.

News accounts do not reveal if John's case against the hospital was successful. He told BBC News that he hoped to settle the case out of court, through arbitration, to spare both himself and the British National Health Service the expense of lawyers. Perhaps he was able to do that. In any case, the story's open ending has a pedagogic advantage: Students can speculate on what a just settlement would be without worrying if their answer is correct.

Unit 4 The Twins of Siam

The term "Siamese twins" originates with Chang and Eng. The preferred term today is "conjoined twins." The phenomenon occurs when a single fertilized egg fails to completely separate into identical twins. It happens once in every 100,000 births, but many conjoined twins do not survive.

Chang and Eng first asked to be separated before their marriages. Doctors said the operation would be dangerous but agreed to try it. The story goes that just as the operation was about to begin, Sarah and Adelaide rushed in to say they loved the twins too much to let them risk their lives. They said they would marry the twins the way they were.

The twins were attracted to rural North Carolina because they liked the landscape and the tolerant people. They bought farmland near the town of Mt. Airy—the real-life inspiration for Andy Griffith's Mayberry—and became gentlemen farmers. When they became U.S. citizens in 1840, they chose the surname "Bunker," the name of some close friends. Many of the descendants of the twins, who had 21 children all together, get together regularly for family reunions. At a recent reunion in Mt. Airy attended by 200 people, one of Eng's great-granddaughters told a reporter from *Newsweek,* "With twins married to two sisters, there is such a 'Bunker look.' It's a small town. Almost everyone is related to the twins."

Unit 5 The Baby Exchange

When Selma brought her baby to the Souzas' house, the two mothers didn't say a word at first; they just hugged each other and sobbed.

Both couples later sued the hospital that gave them the wrong babies.

Unit 6 The Ghost

In the *More True Stories* version of the story, the watch plays the catch-phrase "Come and catch me" from the movie *Spider-Man.* The actual catch-phrase on the watch was "I won't take the *lift* down." (Alfred lives in England, where *lift* is the word for the American English word *elevator*.) American English is standard in the *True Stories* series, so it was decided to replace the phrase "I won't take the lift down" with one entirely in American English. From the phrases commonly found on Spider-Man watches and toys, "Come and catch me" was chosen as the replacement because it was simple and had the bonus of adding more suspense to the story.

The *More True Stories* version of the story differs from the newspaper account in one other detail. It was actually staff members of the local environmental health office who found the source of the quiet voice. In the story, they are identified as "police officers" to make the language more appropriate for the high-beginning level.

Alfred Mansbridge told the *Southern Daily Echo* that during the three months of his ordeal, he never doubted for a minute that there was a rational explanation for the quiet voice. "I don't believe in ghosts," he said, "and I knew I wasn't going mad. This was a genuine mystery."

Unit 7 Why Can't They Quit?

Several teachers characterized this story as a "sleeper story"—one that they expected would not generate much student interest but that turned out to be highly engaging for students who, like Ali, want to quit smoking.

Teaching Tip

In the discussion exercise, students state whether smoking is not allowed in some places in their native countries. Recently, smoking has been outlawed in all public places in some countries and in some U.S. states. That legislation might be an interesting topic for discussion. You could begin the conversation by posting three signs in the classroom: one sign reading "SMOKING PERMITTED IN ALL PUBLIC PLACES"; another reading "SMOKING PERMITTED IN SOME PUBLIC PLACES"; and another reading "SMOKING NOT PERMITTED IN ANY PUBLIC PLACES." Students stand near the sign that most closely expresses their opinion.

Unit 8 Everybody's Baby

The well was 120 feet deep. Jessica went down only 20 feet because it was at that depth that the well narrowed to six inches across.

The men drilled the parallel hole fairly rapidly; by Thursday morning, they were below Jessica and starting to drill the tunnel across to the well. Then they hit solid rock. The rock dulled the diamond-tipped drill bits the men were using, and they progressed at the rate of one inch per hour. At 3 P.M. on Friday, they switched to a high-pressure water drill brought in from Houston and drilled through to the well six hours later. During the last hours of Jessica's 58-hour ordeal, many of the 25 men who were taking turns drilling cried every time they heard Jessica cry.

When an ambulance transported Jessica to the hospital after her rescue, the streets along the route to the hospital were lined with cheering people, and church bells rang.

At first doctors thought they would have to amputate Jessica's right foot, but they were ultimately able to save the foot; only her little toe was amputated. Jessica was in the hospital for one month and had four operations on her foot. An anonymous donor paid her medical bills.

In the photo, Jessica is holding a clump of hair in her left hand. That is her own hair, which she pulled out during her days in the well. The photographer was awarded a Pulitzer Prize for this photo.

A poll taken by the Pew Research Center revealed that in recent decades only the Paris car crash that took Princess Diana's life garnered more worldwide attention than the rescue of Baby Jessica. Jessica and her parents, however, want to live outside the limelight. In a 1997 interview with the *Milwaukee Journal Sentinel* on the tenth anniversary of the rescue, Jessica's mother said, "More than anything, I want her to have a normal childhood. We want everyone to know that she's fine, that she's a healthy, active, loving girl. But we don't want people recognizing her everywhere she goes."

Jessica McClure is married now and has a son. When she is 25 years old, she will gain access to a trust fund that was established for her by well-wishers after her rescue. The fund was originally $267,000 but is estimated to be more than $1 million now.

Unit 9 Pay It Forward

Over the course of 26 years, Larry Stewart gave away 1.3 million dollars in secret; when he gave people money, he never told them his name. Only his family and a few close friends knew about his "hobby." He was known as the "Secret Santa" because he gave the bulk of his money away during the holiday season. Although his unique style of charitable giving was widely reported in the media—*USA Today* profiled him in a front-page story in 2001—newspapers and TV stations respected his desire for anonymity and did not disclose his name. Larry decided to reveal his identity in 2006 when he learned that a tabloid newspaper was going to print it.

After he went public with his philanthropy, Larry got 7,000 e-mails from people all over the world. Many people wrote that he had inspired them to be "Secret Santas," too. One woman wrote that during a recent hotel stay, she had tucked $20 bills into the carts of the housekeeping staff. A man wrote that he went into a discount store with the intention of distributing $100 to shoppers when he met a man who was buying toys to give to needy children. He gave that man the entire amount so that he could buy more toys.

In a 2006 interview with *USA Today*, Larry recounted the story of being given $20 by the owner of the Dixie Diner in Houston, Mississippi. It was only after he had left town that he realized the owner had helped him in a way that wouldn't embarrass him. "Right then I made a promise," Larry recalled. "I said, 'Lord, if you ever put me in a position to help other people, I will.'"

The Associated Press reported that Larry thought "people should know that he was born poor, was briefly homeless, dropped out of college, has been fired from jobs, and once even considered robbery. But he said every time he hit a low point in his life, someone gave him money, food, and hope, and that's why he has devoted his life to returning the favors."

Larry Stewart died of cancer in 2007.

Teaching Tips

A. This story affords the opportunity to introduce the concept of making inferences. Ask students the questions below. Point out that the answers to these questions are *not* in the story and reassure students that any logical answer is correct. Encourage them to begin their answers with the word *maybe*.

1. Why didn't Larry ask his family for help when he ran out of money?

2. Why did Larry tell the restaurant owner, "I lost my wallet" when the man gave him the bill? Why didn't he say, "I'm sorry. I don't have any money"?

3. Why did the restaurant owner say, "I think you dropped this" when he gave Larry the money? Why didn't he just give Larry the money?

4. Why did the waitress cry when Larry gave her $20 and said, "Keep the change"?

B. In the discussion exercise, students talk about people who helped them. The concept of "paying it forward" is another appropriate topic for discussion. On the website of the Random Acts of Kindness Foundation, there are many ideas for paying it forward, including suggestions for classroom activities. A suggested activity that works well with almost any group of students is the following: Each student (as well as the teacher) writes his or her name at the top of a piece of paper. The papers are passed around the classroom, and students write a positive comment about the person whose name is at the top of the page. When all students have written their comments, the papers are returned to their owners.

Unit 10 Please Pass the Bird Brains

In the first edition of *More True Stories*, Queen's Secret, one meal at the restaurant, was described as containing meat from a chicken with black feathers. Several teachers wrote to say that their Chinese students insisted the ingredient was chicken with black *skin*, not black feathers, so the description was changed.

The "dinosaur bones" in Lover's Soup are actually the finely ground fossils of dinosaur bones. They sell for about seven dollars a pound.

Unit 11   Margaret Patrick . . . Meet Ruth Eisenberg

Margaret Patrick began piano lessons when she was eight years old and by age 16 was playing symphony concerts in Harlem. For 30 years, she was organist at churches throughout New York City and Harlem. She told the Hackensack, NJ, *Record*, "After the stroke, I tried to play simple pieces anyway," she said, "but my right hand did what it wanted to. So I would listen to tapes of my concerts to remember."

Ruth Eisenberg learned to play the piano when she was 22 years old and newly married. Her husband, Jacob, wrote textbooks for piano teachers. He asked her to be his student so that he could test his methods. At first Ruth resisted, but then changed her mind when she realized that Jacob did the housework and took care of their children whenever she practiced. Ruth and Jacob traveled all over the country giving demonstrations at schools and universities until Jacob died in 1964. After his death, Ruth played the music Jacob had taught her for several hours a day; it was a source of great comfort to her. Ruth told *Guideposts* magazine that after her stroke, she was despondent. "Music had become the most important thing in my life," she said, "and now all I could do was sit and brood bitterly over the piano I could no longer play."

The two pianists called themselves Ebony and Ivory. Mrs. Eisenberg told the *North Jersey Suburbanite*, "We were great before, but now we are smashing."

Teaching Tips

A. In the discussion exercise, students pair up to find three things they have in common. If your students have trouble getting started, you might want to give them more sample questions, for example:

- What's your favorite color?
- What size shoes do you wear?
- Are you the oldest child in your family?
- Are you a good cook?
- Do you like to watch movies?
- When did you begin to study English?
- Do you have a dog?

B. A whole-group activity is suggested by Gertrude Moskowitz in *Caring and Sharing in the Foreign Language Class*, Heinle and Heinle Publishers, 1978 ("Lots in Common," p. 48). Begin by asking the class a question, such as, "In what month is your birthday?" Students mingle, asking one another, "When is your birthday?" until they find other students who have the same birthday month. Students born in the same month form a group. When all groups are formed, a spokesperson for each group announces the commonality (e.g., "All our birthdays are in May.") Other possible questions to prompt the formation of groups are:

- What time do you get up in the morning?
- What's your favorite season?
- What's your favorite sport?

Unit 12   Finders Keepers?

At first, the Columbus police department hoped the 10% reward would prompt people to turn in money voluntarily. Mel Kiser, the first recipient of the reward, was feted by the mayor, who gave Mr. Kiser tickets to a football game and proclaimed a day in his honor. However, as time went on, and only a few more people came forward with money, the police department decided to get tough. The police announced that people who kept money would be charged with a felony. One police officer told the *Columbus Dispatch*, "A lot of people think it's finders-keepers, like when they were a kid, but this is theft." The police admitted that while filing charges would be easy, the odds of getting convictions were remote.

Months after the truck spilled its cargo, people were still searching along the highway, hoping to find a few stray bills.

Unit 13 The Husband

Giovanni Vigliotto met most of his wives at flea markets, where he went to sell the possessions of previous wives. (He did, however, sometimes deviate from his typical method; on a cruise ship, he met and married four women.) Over the course of 20 years, he married 105 women without divorcing any of them.

After a five-week trial, a jury found him guilty of bigamy and fraud. The Associated Press reported that the jury was "charmed and amazed, but never swayed" as Giovanni told his story of using fifty-one aliases when he married women in 18 U.S. states and 9 foreign countries. Although not a handsome man, he had, in the words of one juror, "some kind of magic about him." In fact, one of the female jurors became infatuated with him and believed that the women who testified against him were lying. The other jurors had to persuade her that Giovanni was the guilty one. He was sent to prison in 1983, at age 53, but did not serve out his 34-year sentence. He died in prison of a brain hemorrhage at age 61.

Teaching Tips

A. In the discussion exercise, students talk about the optimal time couples should know each another before getting married. The story also invites a conversation about qualities that are important in a husband or wife. Remind students that Sharon loved Giovanni because he was intelligent, polite, and kind. Those qualities were important to her. Ask the class to suggest other qualities and write their list on the board. Then have students vote on the three qualities that are most important to them. (Having men and women vote separately

can produce interesting results.) Below is a sample list.

- intelligent
- polite
- kind
- attractive (handsome or pretty)
- honest
- religious
- hard working
- funny
- neat
- generous
- athletic

B. Yet another topic for discussion is the best way to meet a potential spouse. Ask students for ideas and then invite them to weigh in with their opinions. (Some possibilities are: at school, at work, through a mutual friend, through a matchmaker, on a group date, on a website.)

C. If you would like your students to have additional writing practice, you could ask them to imagine the conversation Giovanni and Sharon had over dinner on their first date. Before students write, ask them to work together to create a list of possible topics for the conversation and then, with a partner, compose a conversation between Sharon and Giovanni. Alternately, they could compose a conversation between any two people on their first date. Again, they would first create a list of possible topics before writing.

Unit 14 The Auction

Katie's parents had health insurance, but they were not sure it would cover all of Katie's medical bills.

Katie told the *Columbus Dispatch* that while her lamb was being auctioned, "I stared hard at my dad's face. I was crying. It was great, and it seemed like forever. I didn't know how many times it sold."

Katie's mother said, "The first sale is the only one that I remember, because after that I was crying too hard."

Teaching Tip

An activity that goes nicely with this unit is the sentence auction game. Write about a dozen sentences on the board. Some of the sentences should be grammatically incorrect. For example, you could incorporate the following incorrect sentences into a list of sentences from the story:

- "Today I'm going sell my lamb," she thought.
- People was a little surprised when they saw Katie.
- Katie no had hair.
- Katie wanted sell her lamb and pay some of her medical bills.
- "This young lady need money for her medical bills."
- Then the auctioneer beginned the auction.

Divide students into groups of three or four and give each group $3,000 in play money (or small pieces of candy to use as money). Sell the sentences one by one to the highest bidder. The goal of the game is to buy as many correct sentences as possible. (If the students are playing with candy, the winning team takes the whole pot of "spent" candy.) Bids begin at $200 and increase by $100 each bid. You can heighten the drama of the game by playing your role as auctioneer for all it's worth, saying, for example, "Who will give me $200 for this beautiful short sentence?" There are several variations of the auction game on ESL websites; one credits Mario Rinvolucri as the originator of the game.

Unit 15 Money to Burn

Lillian intended to dry the money for only 40 seconds in her microwave oven, but by force of habit set the timer for five minutes—the time she routinely baked a potato.

The farmer in the story sent the cow's stomach to the Treasury Department because he had been advised to send the money in the container it was destroyed in.

The U.S. Treasury Department will reimburse people the full amount of any damaged bill if their experts can put at least 51% of the bill together.

Teaching Tip

As a follow-up to this story, you could ask students if they have a personal story about losing or finding money in a strange way. They could share their experience in a group or write about it.

Unit 16 The School and the Stamp

In an interview with the *Washington Post*, Rafael Lopez, the Mexican-born San Diego artist who designed the stamp, said, "Like many people, I had never heard of the Mendez case." Indeed, even some members of the Mendez family knew nothing about it. A younger daughter, born several years after the case was decided, was studying Latino history in college when she was astounded to come across her own family's name in a textbook. Until that moment, she had known nothing about the case or her family's role in it.

While Mendez v. Westminster is not nearly as well known as Brown v. the Board of Education, which resulted in the desegregation of schools in the South, in many ways it was a precursor to that more famous case. Some of the key players in the Mendez case would later be prominent figures in the Brown case.

Earl Warren was governor of California when the Mendez case came to trial. Seven years later, as chief justice of the Supreme Court, he wrote the Brown decision. Attorney Thurgood Marshall, who submitted a brief in the Mendez case, later presented similar arguments when he appeared before the Supreme Court in the Brown case.

In a 3/22/2004 interview on NPR's *All Things Considered* (archived under the title "Before Brown v. Board of Education"), Sylvia Mendez, the oldest child, said, "My Dad was so sure we were going to win because he felt that in the United States there was justice . . . there had to be justice." She said that the textbooks they used at the "Mexican school" were hand-me-downs from the other school in Westminster.

A recently built school in Santa Ana, California, was named the Gonzalo and Felicitas Mendez Intermediate School.

Teaching Tips

A. In the comprehension exercise "Understanding the Main Ideas," students complete the answers to the questions. This exercise can subsequently become a small group activity if, after completing the exercise in writing, students ask one another the questions. Teacher Lisa McKinney recommends structuring the activity this way:

1. The teacher asks the first question and calls on a student to read the answer.

2. After reading the answer, that student poses the second question to another student.

3. That student answers the second question and poses the third question to another student, and so on.

Ms. McKinney cautions her students to call on one another by name—no pointing or saying, "You, next." She calls this activity "Pass the Question" and remarks, "There are often grimaces, groans, and lots of grins as students force one another to participate."

B. In the Discussion/Writing exercise, students design a stamp. Ask them to put this information on their stamps: the name of a country, a monetary amount, and a short caption. (For example, a student might add this information: "USA," "42," and "Buckingham Fountain"). There are several websites that give detailed lesson plans for this activity. Some sites give postage stamp templates (with a print-out of a blank stamp), and some give computer-savvy students instructions for designing a stamp using imaging software. Searching under "design a stamp" should yield relevant hits.

C. Another topic for discussion is the issue of separate schools. In the students' native countries, are there separate schools for different religious or ethnic groups? Are there separate schools for girls and boys? Do students attend those schools by choice or by law?

Unit 17 A Long Fishing Trip

The fishermen's five-month ordeal set a world record for survival at sea; the previous record was held by a Chinese sailor who drifted alone in the Atlantic for 133 days during World War II.

The only navigational device that remained on board was the boat's compass, which indicated that the men were heading due west. After two months at sea, the men suspected that they had crossed two time zones because, according to their watches, the sun was setting much later than it had in Costa Rica.

Joel Gonzalez kept his letter to Edith in a little bottle with his wedding ring attached to it. He told *People* magazine, "With my last strength, I was going to throw the bottle into the water, hoping someone would find it and send her the letter."

In the discussion exercise, students guess which job is the most dangerous. The information on dangerous work comes from the U.S. Department of Labor, which compiles statistics on the number of fatal injuries in a particular line of work compared to the percentage of the labor force doing that work in a given year. The rankings vary from year to year. According to figures released in 2008, fisher ranked as the most dangerous occupation, followed by logger, pilot, iron and steel worker, farmer and rancher, roofer, electrical power line installer and repairer, truck driver, refuse and recyclable materials collector, and police officer.

Unit 18 The Surgeon

The San Francisco surgeon who operated on Francisco's hand told *Reader's Digest*, "A thumb without a finger is useless. But a thumb with two fingers provides the pinch that enables you to write or to button a shirt." In a 14-hour operation, a team of eight surgeons took one toe from each of Francisco's feet and attached them to his hand as the ring and pinkie fingers. His post-operative therapy consisted of putting pegs into a pegboard, rolling a rubber ball between his thumb and new fingers, and cutting meat and vegetables into fine pieces.

Before his injury, Dr. Bucio was right handed, but his left hand has become dominant. He uses it to position instruments, while his right hand serves as the helper.

Unit 19 Customer Service?

Mona Shaw believed the employees of the telephone company essentially ignored her concerns. So as she walked around their office, whacking the equipment with a hammer, she repeatedly asked, "Now do I have your attention?"

When police arrived at the office of the phone company, they arrested Mrs. Shaw for disorderly conduct. Later in court she received a three-month suspended sentence, in addition to the $345 fine. She was also barred from entering the company's office for one year. Many people—particularly those who have had similar frustrating disputes with big telecommunications companies—called Mona Shaw a hero. She denied she was a hero. "No, I'm just an old lady who got

mad," she told a reporter from the Associated Press.

Unit 20 The Mermaid Balloon

The MacKinnons, who are themselves the parents of three young daughters, debated for weeks about the best way to reply to Desiree's letter. The letter in the story is the actual letter, slightly abridged to save space, that Mrs. MacKinnon wrote to Desiree.

The story of the mermaid balloon is told in *Mermaid*, a made-for-TV movie starring Ellen Burstyn as Desiree's grandmother. It is widely available on DVD and moderately priced (about $13 dollars as of this writing). The end of the movie (the last 20 minutes or so) is appropriate for classroom viewing. Select chapter 5 of the DVD and search forward to the 1-hour, 08-minute point of the film, when Wade McKinnon finds the balloon while hunting turkeys. (Actually, he was hunting ducks, as the story states). You will, of course, need to preview this section of the movie before showing it. If you do decide to show this movie clip to the class, have a box of tissues ready to pass; the movie is a tear-jerker.

One hundred people at Pittsburgh International Airport were asked, "If you found a balloon with a letter attached to it, would you write to the person who wrote the letter?" Eighty-six of the people said, yes, they would. Responses might be different in other parts of the country, but it is safe to assume that if a student launches a balloon for the writing exercise, and the balloon is found, the chances of getting a reply are good in the United States.

Unit 21 The Two Lives of Mary Sutton

Jenny Cockell finally found Mary's children by writing a letter to the Dublin *Evening Press*. In her letter, she wrote that she was seeking information "relating to the whereabouts of my family, who are the children of John and Mary Sutton of Swords Road, Malahide." One of Mary's granddaughters saw the letter in the newspaper and put Jenny in touch with her father, the second of Mary's sons. Although Mary's children were out of touch, each had just enough information for Jenny to locate another child, until she accounted for all six of the children.

When the four surviving children met with Jenny, they were astonished to hear her describe in great detail their childhood cottage, which had been torn down in 1959. She also described to them a scene she had seen while under hypnosis. She said that the children were upset because they had caught a rabbit in a trap and the rabbit was still alive. She added that it was early morning, and that Sonny, the oldest son, was about 11. Sonny remembered the incident. In her book *Across Time and Death*, Jenny writes: "This was clearly the first piece of information that had really shocked him by its accuracy. The incident was so private to him and his family, how could anyone else know about it?"

Under hypnosis, Jenny Cockell has seen scenes of yet another previous life, of a French country girl who lived in the 1700s, and scenes from a future life, of a Nepalese girl who will be born in the next century.

Some students who participated in field testing this story voiced strong opinions about reincarnation. It might be a good idea to remind students in multicultural classes that the concept of reincarnation is not widely accepted in the West and Middle East but is a commonly held belief in Asia. It is hoped the discussion exercise prompts students to express their opinions, but in a way that is sensitive to classmates who have different religious beliefs.

Unit 22 Two Strangers

After he emerged from under the train, Wesley Autrey refused medical treatment; he said he was fine. Later that day, he went to work. Cameron Hollopeter (whose name was changed to the more easily pronounced name "Peters" for the story) had a few cuts and bruises. He was taken to the hospital for observation and later released. Family members said he had no history of epileptic seizures.

Wesley Autrey became an instant celebrity and was showered with awards and gifts. Among the gifts were $5,000 from the New York Film Academy, where Cameron was a student; $10,000 from Donald Trump; and a week-long trip to Disney World from the Disney Corporation, all expenses paid.

When an interviewer asked Wesley why he had risked his life for a stranger, he replied that he had done it "because I saw a fellow New Yorker in need of help. Why should I stand there and watch that young man die? I wouldn't have felt right in my heart."

As of this writing, there are two short videos on YouTube that are appropriate viewing for the readers of this book. One is David Letterman's interview of Wesley Autrey ("New York Subway Hero, Wesley Autrey"). The other is a segment from the CBS Evening News ("New York Subway Hero, CBS News"). Both video clips include a computer-generated reenactment of the rescue.

Teaching Tip

In the comprehension exercise "Understanding the Main Ideas," students complete the answers to the questions. This exercise can subsequently become a small group activity if, after completing the exercise in writing, students ask one another the questions. Please see the directions for this activity under "Teaching Tip" in Unit 16.

Answer Key

Unit 1

VOCABULARY

2. shivering   3. curious   4. amazed   5. rough

UNDERSTANDING THE MAIN IDEA

1. c   2. b

UNDERSTANDING CAUSE AND EFFECT

2. d   3. b   4. a   5. e

REVIEWING THE STORY

2. came   7. about
3. was   8. distance
4. followed   9. rough
5. swim   10. famous
6. girlfriend 11. love

Unit 2

VOCABULARY

2. trick   3. courthouse   4. wedding   5. punch

UNDERSTANDING THE MAIN IDEA

1. c   2. b

UNDERSTANDING CONNECTIONS

2. d   3. a   4. c

REMEMBERING DETAILS

1. ~~angry~~ / afraid   6. ~~problem~~ / trick
2. ~~brothers~~ / parents   7. ~~library~~ / courthouse
3. ~~party~~ / wedding   8. ~~called~~ / saw
4. ~~boss~~ / friend   9. ~~Bob's~~ / John's
5. ~~Monday~~ / Saturday   10. ~~boyfriend~~ / husband

Unit 3

VOCABULARY

2. c   3. a   4. d   5. b

UNDERSTANDING THE MAIN IDEAS

2. b, c   3. a, c   4. a, b   5. a, b   6. b, c

FINDING INFORMATION

2. two grown children
3. Sally
4. The next day
5. $23,000
6. on the coast of England, in a beautiful area
   (where tourists often visit)
7. at all the best restaurants
8. expensive gifts for his family and friends

UNDERSTANDING A SUMMARY

2

Unit 4

VOCABULARY

2. stare   3. got tired   4. argued

UNDERSTANDING THE MAIN IDEA

1. c   2. b

REMEMBERING DETAILS

2. ~~doctors~~ / twins
3. ~~laugh~~ / stare
4. ~~Australian~~ / American
5. ~~days~~ / years
6. ~~cousins~~ / sisters
7. ~~unhappy~~ / happy
8. ~~can~~ / can't

UNDERSTANDING REASONS

2. d   3. b   4. a   5. c

Unit 5

VOCABULARY

2. b   3. a   4. a

UNDERSTANDING THE MAIN IDEA

1. b   2. c

UNDERSTANDING CAUSE AND EFFECT

2. c   3. d   4. a   5. b

UNDERSTANDING A SUMMARY

1

Unit 6

VOCABULARY

2. widower
3. searched
4. spotted

UNDERSTANDING A SUMMARY

A.
1. police
2. night, quiet
3. living, watch
4. gone, grandson
5. bought, tape
B. Correct order of the sentences: 2, 5, 1, 3, 4

UNDERSTANDING QUOTATIONS

2. d   3. e   4. a   5. b

REMEMBERING DETAILS

1.
He is a widower.
He lives alone.
He has a daughter.
He had trouble sleeping.
He is a grandfather.

2.

It sounded like a ghost or a child.
Alfred heard it every night for 15 seconds.
It said, "Come and catch me."
It repeated the sentence five times.
It woke Alfred up.
It came from a watch.

Unit 7

VOCABULARY

2. pack   3. causes   4. gets used to

UNDERSTANDING THE MAIN IDEA

1. c   2. b

FINDING MORE INFORMATION

2. d   3. a   4. b

REVIEWING THE STORY

2. drug   4. weight 6. little 8. quit   10. way
3. smoking 5. gum   7. chew 9. smoke

Unit 8

VOCABULARY

2. narrow   3. dialed   4. drill   5. injured

UNDERSTANDING THE MAIN IDEA

1. b   2. c

UNDERSTANDING TIME RELATIONSHIPS

2. c   3. e   4. a   5. b

REMEMBERING DETAILS

2. ~~kitchen~~ / yard
3. ~~water~~ / well
4. ~~wrote~~ / dialed
5. ~~cover~~ / hole
6. ~~soft~~ / solid
7. ~~down~~ / up
8. ~~doctors~~ / paramedics
9. ~~old~~ / young
10. ~~days~~ / hours

WRITING

Jessica was playing at a daycare center. Suddenly she fell into a well. She fell about 20 feet and couldn't get out of the well. Men from the fire department came. They couldn't go down into the well because it was too narrow.

    The men decided to drill a hole next to the well. For the next 58 hours, the men drilled the hole. Their job was very difficult because they were drilling through solid rock. Finally they reached Jessica and brought her up from the well. Jessica's foot and forehead were badly injured, but she was alive. Everyone was very happy.

Unit 9

VOCABULARY

2. tank   3. success   4. order   5. change

REVIEWING THE STORY

2. owner   6. bills
3. drove   7. fast-food
4. business   8. more
5. money   9. forward

UNDERSTANDING CAUSE AND EFFECT

2. e   3. a   4. d   5. c

FINDING INFORMATION

2. 22
3. For weeks
4. In a small town in Mississippi
5. He couldn't pay for a hotel room
6. For two days
7. Early in the morning
8. Only one man
9. a big breakfast
10. "I lost my wallet!"

Unit 10

VOCABULARY

2. centuries   3. common   4. digestion

UNDERSTANDING THE MAIN IDEA

1. b   2. a

REMEMBERING DETAILS

2. f   4. a   6. e
3. d   5. g   7. b

FINDING MORE INFORMATION

2. a   3. b   4. c

Unit 11

VOCABULARY

2. d   3. e   4. a   5. c

UNDERSTANDING CONNECTIONS

2. d   3. a   4. f   5. c   6. e

MAKING INFERENCES

2. d   3. a   4. c

UNDERSTANDING A SUMMARY

2

Unit 12

VOCABULARY

2. ripped 3. slammed on their brakes 4. grabbing

REMEMBERING DETAILS

2. ~~bus~~ / truck
3. ~~closed~~ / opened
4. ~~paper~~ / plastic
5. ~~leaves~~ / money
6. ~~houses~~ / cars
7. ~~30~~ / 20
8. ~~tax~~ / reward
9. ~~pennies~~ / dollars

UNDERSTANDING TIME RELATIONSHIPS

2. b   3. a   4. e   5. d

MAKING INFERENCES

2. a   3. e   4. d   5. c

Unit 13

VOCABULARY

2. b   3. f   4. d   5. a   6. c

REMEMBERING DETAILS

~~fruit~~ / flea; ~~new~~ / used; ~~dessert~~ / dinner; ~~weeks~~ /
months; ~~mind~~ / heart; ~~Mexico~~ / Canada; ~~$5,000~~ /
$55,000; ~~car~~ / truck; ~~California~~ / Florida; ~~55~~ / 105

FINDING MORE INFORMATION

2. a   3. d   4. b

UNDERSTANDING TIME AND PLACE

WHEN

at the end of the day
for the next four months
after they got married

WHERE

at the flea market
on the way from Indiana to Canada
at the hotel
all over the United States

Unit 14

VOCABULARY

2. auctioneer   3. chanted   4. cheered

REMEMBERING DETAILS

2. ~~Seven~~ / Seventeen
3. ~~December~~ / July
4. ~~world~~ / county
5. ~~lowest~~ / highest
6. ~~cents~~ / dollars
7. ~~auctioneer~~ / farmer
8. ~~thanked~~ /paid

UNDERSTANDING CAUSE AND EFFECT

2. d   3. a   4. b   5. c

UNDERSTANDING A SUMMARY

2

Unit 15

VOCABULARY

2. refund   3. set the timer   4. experts   5. teller

REMEMBERING DETAILS

She washed it with her jeans.
She put it on the kitchen table to dry.
She burned it in her microwave oven.
She showed it to a teller at the bank.
She sent it to the Treasury Department
She gave it to friends.

UNDERSTANDING PRONOUNS

2. c 3. h 4. d 5. e 6. f 7. a 8. g

UNDERSTANDING A SUMMARY

2

Unit 16

VOCABULARY

2. a   3. c   4. b

UNDERSTANDING THE MAIN IDEAS

1. Mendez
2. farmer, farm worker
3. children, elementary
4. old
5. fight, school
6. close
7. lawyer, court
8. separate, unfair

UNDERSTANDING PRONOUNS

2. d   3. c   4. b   5. e

FINDING INFORMATION

2. when he was a little boy
3. at age ten
4. to become a farm worker
5. Felicitas
6. three
7. a small but successful café
8. in Santa Ana, California

Unit 17

VOCABULARY

2. nets 3. raw 4. survive 5. ran out of

UNDERSTANDING THE MAIN IDEAS

2. b, c 3. a, b 4. a, c 5. a, b

UNDERSTANDING REASONS

2. d   3. e   4. c   5. a

UNDERSTANDING A SUMMARY

2

DISCUSSION

The most dangerous job is fisherman.

Unit 18

VOCABULARY

2. a   3. a   4. a

UNDERSTANDING THE MAIN IDEAS

2. b, c 3. a, b 4. a, b 5. b, c

UNDERSTANDING TIME RELATIONSHIPS

2. d   3. c   4. a   5. b

UNDERSTANDING A SUMMARY

1

Answer Key

Unit 19

VOCABULARY

2. What if
3. damage
4. don't mind

UNDERSTANDING THE MAIN IDEAS

1. c   2. a   3. b

REMEMBERING DETAILS

1.
She usually lives a quiet life.
She lives in a suburb of Washington, D.C.
She is 75 years old.
She has a bad heart.
She is married.

2.
On Monday she waited all day for the technician, but he didn't come.
The technician disconnected her old phone service, but he couldn't connect her new service.
Mona waited for two hours to talk to the manager.
A company representative told Mona, "Someone will come to your house next Tuesday," but nobody came.

UNDERSTANDING WORD GROUPS

lamp, cook, teacher

Unit 20

VOCABULARY

2. b   3. a   4. a

UNDERSTANDING THE MAIN IDEA

1. b   2. b

REMEMBERING DETAILS

2. ~~fish~~ / mermaid
3. ~~Arizona~~ / California
4. ~~south~~ / east
5. ~~years~~ / days
6. ~~mountain~~ / lake
7. ~~feeding~~ / hunting
8. ~~cake~~ / present

FINDING MORE INFORMATION

2. c   3. a   4. d

Unit 21

VOCABULARY

2. barn   3. surviving   4. childhood

UNDERSTANDING THE MAIN IDEA

1. b   2. c

FINDING MORE INFORMATION

2. b   3. c   4. a   5. d   6. f

REMEMBERING DETAILS

2. M   6. M
3. M   7. J
4. J   8. M
5. J

Unit 22

VOCABULARY

2. c   3. e   4. a   5. d

UNDERSTANDING THE MAIN IDEAS

2. fell, tracks
3. lights
4. heavier, feet
5. between, tracks
6. hat
7. fifth
8. them

UNDERSTANDING TIME RELATIONSHIPS

2. e   3. d   4. c   5. a

FINDING INFORMATION

2. four and six
3. New York City
4. construction worker
5. on the second shift
6. home (from school)

Acknowledgments

I WISH TO THANK:

- the many teachers who have e-mailed me or sought me out at TESOL conventions to tell me about their experiences with the *True Stories* books. I am grateful for your feedback, which helps me assess how the stories and exercises are working outside the small sphere of my own classroom. Your suggestions are always welcome;

- my students at the American Language Institute, Indiana University of Pennsylvania, and at Whitewater (WI) Community Education, who gave me their honest opinions of the stories and who provided the writing samples and drawings;

- Peggy Miles, who field-tested materials at the Santa Cruz (CA) Adult School;

- my former colleague Sharron Bassano, who read an early version of the manuscript and whose comments were, as always, astute. The writing exercise in Unit 4 and the discussion exercise in Unit 8 reflect the influence of her teaching style;

- Pietro Alongi, whose expert editorial help during the early stages of writing improved the new stories;

- Karen Davy, whose skilled and experienced hands guided this book through its middle stages;

- Dana Klinek, whose calm and steady hands guided this book through its final stages;

- Akiya Miyazato, editor-in-chief of the *Ryukyu Shimpo*, Arthur Porter, editor of the *Bridlington Free Press*, and the many newspaper librarians and reporters who provided clippings, photos, and leads;

- Ichiro Tabeshita, Yuko Yamagishi, Hiroko Mizumori, and Kaoru Nakahori, who translated materials for "Puppy Love'";

- Zilda de Moura and Sharon Miranda, who translated materials for "The Baby Exchange";

- Anna Silliman, editor of *Hands-on English*, who sent me the "one question interview idea of Fiona Armstrong, Adult Basic Education, New York City Schools (used in Unit 5);

- Hong Kun and Zhang Xiaolin, who offered their viewpoints on Chinese medicinal food;

- Margaret Patrick, who sent her collection of clippings;

- Trish Moore and Rhonda Gill, grandmother and mother of Desiree, the little girl who launched the mermaid balloon, who gave permission to include their amazing story in this book;

- Laurel Pollard and Natalie Hess, authors of *Zero Prep* (Alta Book Center Publishers, 1997). The discussion/writing exercise in Unit 22 is based on an activity in that book ("People We Admire," p. 3);

- Kathy Olson, who demonstrated several of the post-reading activities suggested in the To the Teacher section at TESOL 2007 (in a presentation titled "Repetition: Multiple Activities Using One Reading Selection");

- Penny Ur and Andrew Wright, who describe the "Disappearing Summary" activity suggested in the To the Teacher section in their teacher resource book *Five-Minute Activities* (Cambridge University Press, 1992) and who in turn credit the activity to Michael Buckby;

- Roxie Daggett, Santa Fe (NM) Community College, who contributed the activity for teaching vocabulary with gestures and who credits colleague Jenny Sanborn with inspiring the idea;

- Seung-hyun Kim, who provided the drawing for Unit 8;

- Antonia Villalva and Ximena Torres, who provided the writing examples for Units 9, 13, and 22.